PICTURE YOURSELF
Going Green

Step-by-Step Instruction for Living a Budget-Conscious,
Earth-Friendly Lifestyle in Eight Weeks or Less

Erinn Morgan

COURSE TECHNOLOGY
CENGAGE Learning™

Picture Yourself Going Green
Erinn Morgan

**Publisher and General Manager,
Course Technology PTR:** Stacy L. Hiquet

Associate Director of Marketing: Sarah Panella

Manager of Editorial Services: Heather Talbot

Marketing Manager: Jordan Casey

Acquisitions Editor: Megan Belanger

Project Editor: Jenny Davidson

Technical Reviewer: Douglas Schnitzspahn

PTR Editorial Services Coordinator: Jen Blaney

Interior Layout: Shawn Morningstar

Cover Designer: Mike Tanamachi

Indexer: Sharon Shock

Proofreader: Laura Gabler

For product information and technology assistance, contact us at

**Cengage Learning Customer and Sales Support,
1-800-354-9706**

For permission to use material from this text or product, submit all requests online at
cengage.com/permissions

Further permissions questions can be emailed to
permissionrequest@cengage.com

Library of Congress Control Number: 2008935091
ISBN-13: 978-1-59863-844-8
ISBN-10: 1-59863-844-0

Course Technology, a part of Cengage Learning
20 Channel Center Street
Boston, MA 02210
USA

Cengage Learning is a leading provider of customized learning solutions with office locations around the globe, including Singapore, the United Kingdom, Australia, Mexico, Brazil, and Japan. Locate your local office at:
international.cengage.com/region

Cengage Learning products are represented in Canada by Nelson Education, Ltd.

For your lifelong learning solutions, visit **courseptr.com**
Visit our corporate website at **cengage.com**

Printed in the United States of America
1 2 3 4 5 6 7 11 10 09

For my noble grandfather, Charles Theodore Woll,
who taught me the value of hard work, the joy of laughter,
and the beauty of conserving our natural resources.

Acknowledgments

WHEN I BEGAN THIS PROCESS, I never knew what a true team effort it would become. As such, there are many kind, diligent, and talented souls to thank. I must applaud former Course PTR Editorial Assistant Erin Johnson for believing in this concept and pursuing it with such passion. A giant thanks to Acquisitions Editor Megan Belanger for propagating the enthusiasm and exhibiting great patience when the deadlines loomed large. And kudos to Project Editor Jenny Davidson for doing such a fine job of editing, encouraging, and keeping it all flowing smoothly.

I must also thank my friend Doug Schnitzspahn, a talented journalist and editor, for his tireless assistance as the technical editor for this book. His in-depth knowledge of environmental and green issues, garnered in part from his own website initiative www.sustainabler.com, was a tremendous boon to this tome and his input is infused throughout the chapters.

A special thanks to my husband Darren, whose patience helped encourage my own perseverance in completing this behemoth project. His green nature has inspired me since the day we met, from his zeal for composting and recycling to his commitment to reusable bags and his ever-increasing awareness of water conservation as he watches his Australian family suffer year after year of worsening drought conditions.

I also thank my parents, the writer and the English teacher, who helped with everything from research and background information to mental support. The small steps they make every day to green their own lives are inspiring to me.

I am also grateful to my research assistant Stacy Falk for her tireless and diligent exploration of the latest green developments and to my good friend Jody Furtney who, even in the face of adversity, found time to help me with information when I needed it most.

Because of the help of all these people, *Picture Yourself Going Green* has transitioned from a small seed of an idea to become a full reality. We hope you enjoy it…

About the Author

Durango, Colorado-based journalist ERINN MORGAN is an award-winning magazine editor who relocated from New York City to the Southwest five years ago to be closer to Mother Nature, live a more sustainable lifestyle, and launch a freelance writing career. Her written work, which focuses on outdoor adventure and eco-conscious living, has appeared in numerous publications, including *The New York Times*, *Outside* magazine, *National Geographic Adventure*, *Skiing*, *Bike*, and *Natural Solutions*, plus on www.greenlivingideas.com. Erinn is also the editor of *Cleaning Green* magazine.

She focuses on sustainable living, in part, by reducing, reusing, and recycling on a day-to-day basis. She and her husband also practice energy-saving measures and use toxin-free products at home plus buy local and organic foods, grow some of their own food, use renewable energy at home, and telecommute to work. They also recently planned and held their own green-themed, carbon-neutral wedding on the banks of the Colorado River in Utah's canyon country.

Table of Contents

Introduction

MY 84-YEAR-OLD GRANDMOTHER grew up during the Great Depression. To this day, she reuses paper towels after they dry out, turns off the lights when she leaves a room, cleans and reuses Ziploc bags, washes her plates and glasses in a dish tub, and leads a generally minimalist lifestyle.

Today, these efforts are considered trendy and green by a modern generation that is looking to help save the planet. To her generation, they were merely conserving resources and saving money.

She recently explained to me that her family was lucky during the Depression because they lived near farms and always had food during those challenging times. Today, much of our food is shipped to us from thousands of miles away and going to the farmer's market and, thus, supporting local farms is a novelty. Just how sustainable is the world in which we live?

It is possibly the quest for "more" that has led us to stray so far from the unknowingly planet-conscious ideals of my grandmother's generation in the span of several decades. More food, more clothing, more variety, more stuff, bigger houses, better cars, more incredible far-flung vacations.

And now we face the future, fully loaded down with all the baggage of more—and a planet that is reaching out for help—as our society begins to contemplate the ideal that "less" might actually, finally and unequivocally, be "more." Which is exactly where the concept of Going Green comes into play.

Going Green is a noble quest that lies, generally, in the tenets of "less"—conserving resources and reducing, reusing, and recycling. It is taking care of the planet by minimizing our own impact, whether that is accomplished by screwing in a few energy-saving compact fluorescent light bulbs or driving a gas-efficient hybrid automobile. It also hones in on reducing fossil fuel consumption to limit our climate-changing carbon dioxide emissions.

Going Green, with all of its vintage appeal, also has a decidedly modern twist. Today, Going Green does involve simple steps, like those my grandmother's generation does naturally, such as conserving kitchen supplies, water, and energy. But it also puts the onus on protecting our own health (and the health of our family) by doing what we can to limit our exposure to the complex brew of chemicals, many of which remain unregulated, in everything from our foods and personal care products to clothing and children's toys. As it turns out, Going Green is also good for our health.

With a few exceptions, Going Green is also an effort that will save you money. By doing things like conscientiously turning off lights, notching the thermostat down one degree, carpooling to work, putting the right tire pressure in your auto's wheels, and taking a slightly shorter shower, you can actually save a whole lot of cash. In today's turbulent economic times, this may come as a welcome relief.

The beauty of Going Green is that it can also be so very simple. If you can make even the smallest change, like buying an organic peach or turning off the water while you brush your teeth, you have gone green. Welcome to the party.

I feel very honored to have been chosen to write this book, especially at a time in history when the green movement is picking up incredible speed. It has opened my eyes even further and made my lifestyle significantly greener. When I started writing this book, I thought I was green. What I learned was that I still had much more to learn. And, that I will take a lesson from the unwritten book drawn up by my grandmother's generation, one of the greenest manifestos around.

By following some or all of the simple steps outlined in this book, you will be making a significant contribution to help resolve some of the most pressing problems that plague our planet and its peoples today. I hope you enjoy your green journey—know that each simple change you undertake will make a difference.

Going Green Cost Meter

To help you understand the costs involved with each green step that is presented here, this book is equipped with a dollar sign key:

$ = $0 to $25

$ $ = $25 to $50

$ $ $ = $50 to $100

$ $ $ $ = $100 and up

Extra Information

A variety of sidebar boxes, which present key earth-conscious information, are also delivered throughout the book:

 Eco Fact: pertinent information, often statistical in nature, about environmental hazards and the green movement.

 Green Idea: inspiring details on new projects, developments, and initiatives that are green in nature.

 Green on the Cheap: information on inexpensive ways you can green your lifestyle.

Green is the future

What Is Green?

WE LIVE IN FASCINATING TIMES. As many of the world's inhabitants begin to move in concert to green their lives, their businesses, and their governments, this eco-conscious movement is picking up incredible speed. Seemingly on a daily basis, it is changing the landscape of the earth and the culture of its peoples.

As such, there has never been a better time to go green. Today, there are more earth-friendly tools, resources, products, concepts, and passionate organizations than ever before. Living green does not have to involve lots of sacrifice. In fact, a quest to green your lifestyle can be exciting, adventurous, and fun.

But, green may not be exactly what you think it is. There is a new collective consciousness on this horizon; one that has shaped a different definition of "green." What is this new green? It's all about respecting and caring for the planet *plus* caring for our own health by reducing the amount of harmful chemicals that enter our bodies and our waterways. Going green is good for the longevity of all parties involved.

The best part, given our turbulent economic times, is that going green is affordable. In fact, in most cases making your life more earth-friendly will absolutely save you money in the long run. Who doesn't want to save some green?

This book's eight-week plan will help you green the key—and most impactful—facets of your life. It will help you trim down your own personal carbon footprint—the measure your activities have on the environment in terms of greenhouse gas emissions. *Picture Yourself Going Green* includes simple, budget-conscious steps to green your home, energy use, and the food you eat, plus your yard, wardrobe, personal care products, transportation, and travel. But, first we take a look at why going green is so important for you, your family, and the planet.

Green Is Necessary

WHILE GOING GREEN CAN be an attractive transition for your lifestyle, it is also a sheer necessity for the health of Planet Earth. It's highly likely that you've heard of "global warming," but did you know that scientists have concluded that the earth's average surface air and ocean temperature rose by 1.33 degrees Fahrenheit from 1905 to 2005? The Intergovernmental Panel on Climate Change (IPCC) has determined that this change was, unequivocally, the result of increased levels of greenhouse gases in our atmosphere.

Scientists project that global warming will cause severe drought and unusual weather patterns.
©istockphoto.com/Clint Spencer

Where do greenhouse gases come from? The majority are caused by human activities such as the generation of electricity and the use of gasoline for driving, both activities that burn fossil fuels and emit CO_2. In fact, the average American is responsible for emitting over 21 tons of carbon dioxide per year. Beyond climate change, these gases also contaminate our air and cause pollution-related health problems around the world.

When these emissions rise up to the atmosphere, they cause the "greenhouse effect," which is a process that involves the absorption and emission of infrared radiation by atmospheric gases. Ultimately, this activity traps heat in the atmosphere, which causes the temperature of the planet's lower atmosphere and surface to rise.

We are already seeing what a change of just over one degree in temperature has wrought—from the melting of polar ice caps to the increase in severe weather patterns like hurricanes, drought, and flood. In 2008, the 4,500-year-old Markham Ice Shelf broke away from Ellesmere Island in Canada's northern Arctic, illustrating the planet-altering effects of climate change. This 19-square-mile ice sheet, which is about the size of Manhattan, is now floating unanchored in the Arctic Ocean.

If the people, industries, and governments of the earth do nothing to curb the current rate of greenhouse gas emissions, the projection is dire. The IPCC predicts the average surface temperature of the earth will likely rise another 2 to 11.5 degrees Fahrenheit by the end of the 21st century. This dramatic shift would more than turn up the heat—the effects would start at agriculture-killing drought, the spread of disease, and mass species extinction. According to the U.S. Geological Survey, thinning sea ice caused by global warming could kill off two-thirds of the world's polar bear population by 2050.

Where will the polar bears go when the ice sheets melt?
©istockphoto.com/Jan Will

As you can see, the planet needs your assistance. Simple steps, such as conserving electricity in your home or choosing to drive less, will help tremendously. If each capable person makes a few switches, the impact could be strong enough to change our course and the fate of the planet.

While climate change is certainly a major impetus behind the green movement, there is also a growing concern about the dwindling nature of our natural resources, namely non-renewable fossil fuels such as oil and natural gas. Fossil fuels are a result of the compression and heating of ancient organic matter underneath the earth's surface. At some point in time, our society will fully exhaust the global supply of fossil fuels, having burned them up in our vehicles and our homes' energy sources.

Oil, in particular, is a topic of hot debate today as many experts believe we will soon reach "peak oil," a point where the world's rate of extraction of this resource will begin to decline quickly, even as our demand increases. Some scientists believe this day of reckoning may have already come, a fact that is underscored by statistics that show flat levels of world oil production over the last few years.

Oil production in the U.S. has already reached its peak.
©istockphoto.com/Mark Evans

Eco Fact

Even as many people try to curb their climate-changing actions, the world's amount of carbon dioxide emissions continued to rise in 2007. According to an annual report from the Global Carbon Project, emissions grew by 3 percent from 2006. It also noted that, for the first time, developing nations took the lead in CO_2 emissions. For instance, China, which was responsible for 60 percent of the world's overall rise in CO_2 emissions, was found to be the largest carbon dioxide polluter. As a country, the U.S. is currently responsible for the second-largest amount of greenhouse gas emissions.

What would we do without oil? It's a scenario that is hard to imagine, especially since the U.S. is the largest consumer of this fossil fuel. While the demand is high—we use over 20 million barrels per day—the U.S. only produced about 7.6 million barrels a day in 2005. This reality means that well over 50 percent of America's oil is imported from other countries.

If oil production does in fact peak, this will cause the cost of gas to skyrocket along with the prices of consumer goods, from food to home supplies. Some project this event could cause widespread poverty, hunger, and even war. Again, it will be your green resourcefulness that can help assuage the effects of a waning oil supply. As the world amps up with alternative energies and cutting-edge hybrid and electric vehicle technology, you can do your part by simply trying to conserve resources.

Green Is Inspiring

WHILE THE PROBLEMS WE FACE are undoubtedly daunting and even somewhat frightening, there is a concept that supersedes even the emissions, the pollution, and the resource crunch. That concept is the power, perseverance, and ingenuity being demonstrated by members of the human race. From those who simply do their part to recycle to those who champion the development of renewable energies, the world is in motion—and on the path to resolution.

As we watch the world turning greener every day, the excitement is infectious; more and more people are buying organic, swapping out traditional light bulbs for energy-saving compact fluorescent lamps (CFLs), and even choosing to drive hybrid vehicles. Even as some federal governments remain reticent about the need to address climate change and peak oil via regulations and laws, states, cities, and even small towns are taking matters into their own hands.

For example, in 2008, Chicago mayor Richard Daley unveiled a groundbreaking plan for the Windy City to dramatically cut its greenhouse gas emissions in an effort to do its part to protect the planet. The Chicago Climate Action Plan calls for the reduction of emissions to three-fourths of 1990 levels by 2020 via the use of clean, renewable energy sources, reducing industrial pollution, and more energy-efficient buildings.

Offshore wind power is one exciting wave of the future.
©istockphoto.com/luismmolina

As the country waits for the U.S. government to deliver a future-altering plan to address emissions, some states are stepping up to the plate. The Regional Greenhouse Gas Initiative (RGGI) is an effort by a group of 10 states in the Northeastern U.S. to reduce greenhouse gas emissions by implementing a cap and trade system to regulate CO_2 emissions from power plants. "Cap and trade" basically equates to a cap being set on emissions and those that emit more must buy (or "trade") credits from those that emit less than their allowance. If regulated worldwide, emissions trading could potentially quell global warming.

Even companies are jumping into the fray with green efforts and ideas. Google.org, the philanthropic arm of the search engine behemoth, has delivered an inspiring plan to move the U.S. to a future of clean energy, from electricity to transportation. It proposes that by 2030, electricity will be generated by wind, solar, and geothermal power. The $4.4 trillion plan also suggests that 90 percent of all new vehicles sold will be plug-in hybrids.

The world is abuzz with the green movement. Are you inspired yet?

Green Idea

Is God green? So sayeth Interfaith Power & Light, a non-partisan ministry that advocates the greening of places of worship; it says if the country's estimated 300,000 churches reduced energy use by 25 percent, it would prevent more than five million tons of CO_2 emissions. Even conservative religious leaders have joined the green cause—the Evangelical Climate Initiative calls for federal legislation to reduce CO_2 emissions via a cap and trade system. It also calls on Christians to take action to combat global warming by conserving energy and supporting green businesses.

Green Is Healthy

THE NEW-AND-EXPANDED definition of "green" also encompasses the preservation of your own health—and that of the planet and its ecosystems. This job has become increasingly difficult in modern times, as the developed world is quite clearly living in the Chemical Age, where harmful ingredients are used in everything from the pesticides that coat our foods to the sunscreens we apply to our children.

A whopping one billion pounds of pesticides are used in the U.S. each year, most of which are sprayed on food crops. These chemicals, many of which are considered toxic and carcinogenic, end up on our dinner plates, in school lunches, and even in our baby foods. One of the most potent is the pesticide diazinon, which was developed as a nerve gas in World War II; it has been banned from residential use because of its health risks to children but is still approved for use on farm crops.

To the rescue comes the organic food movement, which helps keep pesticides out of our bodies and our waterways—these chemicals have also been found in streams, rivers, and surface waters where they disturb the environment and harm wildlife. Organic foods, from produce to meats and milk products, rely on farming methods that eliminate the use of pesticides and deliver more humane treatment to animals.

Organic foods have also been proven to contain more nutrients than conventionally produced foods. A 2008 report that compared 236 foods grown organically with those grown traditionally found that organic foods contain, on average, 25 percent higher concentration of 11 nutrients than their conventional counterparts. Overwhelming demand by a public that wants healthier foods for their families has made organic options more readily available today than ever before.

A healthier, chemical-free earth is possible.
©istockphoto.com/Julien Grondin

An amazing brew of harmful chemicals also makes its way into our personal care products, from toothpaste and hand cream to makeup and deodorant. The most surprising fact of this issue is that our government does not regulate this industry, or the ingredients it packs into our products, on any level.

According to a study conducted by the Environmental Working Group (EWG), the average adult uses nine personal care products each day, altogether concocted with an average of 126 chemical ingredients, many of them harmful as they enter our bloodstreams and our waterways as they get washed down the sink. Excellent information from groups like the EWG, plus the availability of natural personal care options, has made it a whole lot easier to protect your own health and the earth on which you live.

Eco Fact

A 2008 report in the journal *Science* revealed that ocean dead zones, which have too little oxygen to support sea life, have reached an alarming number. With 400 now found in the world's oceans, scientists are pinning the blame on pollution-fed algae, which is caused primarily by fertilizers and other farm run-off, sewage, and the burning of fossil fuels.

Green Is Affordable

AS THE CHAPTERS OF THIS book unfold, you will find that going green is, in fact, a budget-boosting lifestyle choice that will ultimately save you money on many fronts. Conserving resources at home will make you greener *and* enable you to realize real savings on your electricity, water, and natural gas bills. Choosing to drive more efficiently or even drive less by biking to work or taking mass transit will not only lower your carbon footprint, it will also shave a significant amount off your yearly fuel bills. In fact, the average commuter could save as much as $3,000 in vehicle costs each year by choosing to carpool.

Will you celebrate these savings in today's challenging economic and social times? A number of eco-conscious people are already doing so with excellent results. Making a switch as simple as replacing a few of your traditional light bulbs with energy-efficient compact fluorescent lamps (CFLs) could save you hundreds of dollars in energy bills. Even though CFLs can cost three to four times more than incandescent bulbs (they range from about $6 to $7 each), they last about 10 to 15 times longer. As such, it is estimated that homeowners will save $30 or more in electricity costs over each bulb's lifetime. This fact means that a house full of CFLs will save you a substantial amount of money in the long run.

The tenets of green, which include the three Rs of reducing, reusing, and recycling, will also save money. Reducing what you need and buy certainly saves your hard-earned dollars. Reusing things like shopping bags and water bottles also keeps the cash in your wallet while keeping trash out of our growing landfills. Recycling also eliminates an entire waste stream from the world's problematic landfills; it could also make you some money if your area offers a buy-back center.

Installing CFLs in your home will reap significant savings on your energy bill.
©istockphoto.com/Kais Tolmats

Some green changes, such as buying organic foods or natural, chemical-free personal care products, may cost you a little bit more. But, the peace of mind gained from these purchasing decisions will more than make up for the extra money spent. The beauty of going green is that it will ultimately save you money *and* make your life more sustainable at the same time.

Let us leave them a better place.
©istockphoto.com/eva serrabassa

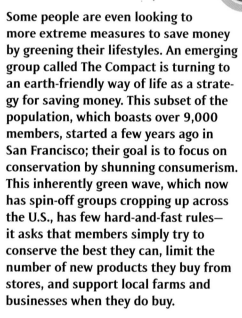

Green on the Cheap

Some people are even looking to more extreme measures to save money by greening their lifestyles. An emerging group called The Compact is turning to an earth-friendly way of life as a strategy for saving money. This subset of the population, which boasts over 9,000 members, started a few years ago in San Francisco; their goal is to focus on conservation by shunning consumerism. This inherently green wave, which now has spin-off groups cropping up across the U.S., has few hard-and-fast rules— it asks that members simply try to conserve the best they can, limit the number of new products they buy from stores, and support local farms and businesses when they do buy.

Green Is the Future

THERE IS AN AMERICAN Indian principle from The Great Law of the Iroquois Confederacy that lays out resonant words to live by, especially given today's challenges:

"In our every deliberation, we must consider the impact of our decisions on the next seven generations."

This code of conduct also inspired the company name of the earth-friendly products producer Seventh Generation. More than ever, now is the time to consider the future of our children and all those who follow them.

What kind of stage are we setting for the coming generations? What kind of planet will they inherit? And, will they look back upon us as the heroic society that turned things around when the planet stood up and asked for help?

There is an island called Samsø sitting alone off the coast of Denmark that has seen the future. Just over a decade ago, islanders got their power from coal-fueled electricity supplied by the mainland, plus oil and petrol shipped in on tankers. Today, its population of 4,100 now lives in the greenest, cleanest, and largest carbon-neutral settlement on the planet.

After winning a national contest to become Denmark's model community for cutting carbon emissions and upping sustainable energy resources, Samsø devoted itself to launching a renewable energy revolution. It would eventually build and produce enough wind, solar, and biomass power to cut its carbon footprint by 140 percent. This small island currently creates enough energy for its own needs and exports the surplus to the mainland.

What is your future? Earth-conscious living is attainable today on all levels of the spectrum. You have already made the first step towards a greener, more sustainable lifestyle by setting out to read this book. Following the simple steps ahead will be your honorable contribution to doing the right thing for your family, the earth, and the next seven generations.

Where is your carbon footprint heading?
©istockphoto.com/Daniel Cooper

It's easy being green.

Ten Simple Steps

GOT TIME TO GO GREEN? Working Americans squeeze only an average of five hours of leisure time out of every day, according to a 2007 Bureau of Labor Statistics study. So, while going green may be appealing, you might just be wondering how you can fit it into your busy lifestyle.

This book outlines a simple, step-by-step process that can make your life more earth-friendly in a matter of eight short weeks with a reasonable time commitment. But, if you are anxious to make key changes right away or don't have the time right now to implement a two-month plan, then this chapter is just for you.

The ten quick, easy changes laid out here will make your lifestyle more eco-conscious immediately. Do you have time to toss your soda cans in the recycle bin? Or choose organic delectables in your grocery store's produce department? Can you bring a reusable grocery bag on your shopping trips? You can incorporate these uncomplicated switches in a snap and, at the same time, make a world of difference. Together, along with the large collective of individuals who are making these acts a regular part of their repertoire, we can work to save the planet.

1. Recycle
2. Install Energy-Saving Light Bulbs
3. Drink from a Reusable Water Bottle
4. Tote a Reusable Shopping Bag
5. Buy Green Power

6. Buy Carbon Offsets
7. Add Organic Food into Your Diet
8. Take a Five-Minute Shower
9. Unplug at Home
10. Plant a Tree

1. Recycle

THE AVERAGE AMERICAN tosses seven-and-a-half pounds of garbage each and every day. Where does it all end up? If you're not recycling, then most of this refuse (that's more than a ton at 2,700 pounds per person a year) ends up in a landfill to be compacted and buried—or in our oceans.

A Whole Lot of Rubbish

The world's largest landfill is called the Great Pacific Garbage Patch, and it encompasses two large floating debris fields located in the Northern Pacific Ocean between Japan and the U.S. This is no man-made dumpsite. Its mass, which is twice the size of the continental U.S., has been formed over several decades within the North Pacific Gyre, the center of a series of swirling currents several thousand miles wide that trap a laundry list of rubbish including bottles, plastic bags, clothing, and fishnets.

Plastic is the main ingredient in this synthetic soup and it now outnumbers the Gyre's marine food source, zooplankton, by 6:1. The problem is that modern plastics do not biodegrade. Instead, they photodegrade in sunlight, becoming brittle and breaking into smaller pieces that are mistaken by birds and other marine life for food—often a deadly error. In addition to killing wildlife by ingestion or entanglement, plastics and other floating debris are also polluting our oceans and putting toxins into our water. This plastic is now passing through the food chain from fish to birds to mammals and, ultimately, to humans.

An astounding amount of trash is floating in our oceans.
©istockphoto.com/jacus

You can make a huge difference in the future of our planet by choosing to recycle. This simple act will reduce waste in our oceans and landfills, reduce energy usage for manufacturing (i.e., manufacturing with recycled aluminum cans uses 95 percent less energy), and also help prevent global warming. In fact, the National Recycling Coalition says the recycling of solid waste in 2001 prevented the release of 32.9 million metric tons of carbon equivalent into the air.

Toss It in the Bin

While recycling in the U.S. has become a $236-billion-a-year industry, an estimated 75 percent of what Americans throw into the trash could still be recycled, according to the Environmental Protection Agency (EPA).

Twenty years ago, there was only one curbside recycling program in the U.S.; today, curbside recycling serves more than half the U.S. population. If your city doesn't offer this pickup service, there are three other primary methods of collection for recyclables, including drop-off centers, buy-back centers, and deposit/refund programs.

If you have access to curbside recycling, you're in luck—take the simple step to join in your area's program via the city office. You will receive a recycling bin (or bins) along with instructions on separating out items like glass, plastic, and paper. Expanded recycling options may exist where you live, but according to Earth911, the most commonly included materials are The Big Five—aluminum, glass, paper, plastic, and steel.

If curbside hasn't made it your way yet, don't worry, many communities feature easily accessed drop-off recycling stations or buy-back centers, the latter of which actually will buy back a variety of your recyclables. Finally, availability of deposit/refund programs vary greatly by region; if available, you can turn in things like bottles, cans, and tires to recoup the nominal deposit paid when the item was purchased.

Separate recycling bins help you divide up items like paper, plastic, and glass. ©stockphoto.com/sweetym

To pinpoint what types of services are available within your specific zip code, log onto www.Earth911.org. You can also contact your city's resident services office directly to see what is offered in your area.

2. Install Energy-Saving Light Bulbs

SHINE A LIGHT ON YOUR green nature by replacing some or all of your home's traditional incandescent light bulbs with newer, energy-efficient compact fluorescent lamps (CFLs), which use 75 percent less energy. Doing so will help you save on your energy bills, reduce greenhouse gas emissions, and put your household ahead of the curve.

The Energy Independence and Security Act of 2007 (a.k.a. the "Energy Bill"), signed by President Bush, requires that all light bulbs use 30 percent less energy than today's incandescent bulbs by 2012 to 2014. By 2020, all bulbs will be required to be at least 70 percent more efficient (equal to today's CFLs).

Energy-efficient compact fluorescent lamps (CFLs) can be screwed into a regular light socket.
©istockphoto.com/Kais Tolmats

Eco Fact

According to the government's ENERGY STAR program, if every homeowner in the U.S. replaced just one light bulb with an ENERGY STAR qualified bulb, together we would shave off more than $600 million in annual energy costs, save enough energy to light more than three million homes for an entire year, and prevent greenhouse gases equivalent to the emissions of more than 800,000 cars.

The National Resource Defense Council (NRDC) estimates that this law could cut our nation's electric bill by more than $10 billion a year. CFLs will not be the "required" bulbs, per se, if other technology is developed in this timeframe. But why not get a jumpstart today?

Since lighting costs represent about 20 percent of the average U.S. household's energy bill, buying and installing energy-efficient CFLs in your home could save you a substantial amount of money in the long run. These bulbs cost about three to four times more than incandescent bulbs, but they last about 10 to 15 times longer. ENERGY STAR estimates that homeowners will save about $30 or more in electricity costs over each bulb's lifetime.

Choose ENERGY STAR qualified CFLs labeled "warm white" or "soft white" to get light similar to that given off by incandescent bulbs. Most home improvement retailers in your area will carry a range of CFLs to fit almost every lighting need. If you cannot find a CFL to fit a specific lighting need, simply try to turn this light off when not in use or consider installing an energy-saving dimmer switch on this fixture—any light bulb dimmed by 25 percent will use about 20 percent less energy.

Today's CFLs do contain a small amount of mercury and the EPA recommends that consumers handle the bulbs accordingly (i.e., with care not to break) and recycle them at appropriate locations. These can be located by checking out epa.gov/bulbrecycling or www.earth911.org.

IKEA offers a recycling program for CFLs, and Home Depot recently announced that it would also collect the bulbs. The company also moved the light-fixture showrooms in its nearly 2,000 stores over to CFLs in 2008, a move that is expected to save upwards of $16 million annually in energy costs.

3. Drink from a Reusable Water Bottle

TODAY, OUR SOCIETY consumes a tremendous amount of bottled water. Americans drink more than seven billion gallons a year, almost all of which comes packaged in polyethylene terephthalate (PET) plastic.

Unfortunately, only about 23 percent of these plastic water bottles are recycled in the U.S. the other 38 billion pile up in landfills across the country and float in our oceans. Of the 100 million tons of plastics produced each year, an unbelievable 10 percent ends up in the sea. Experts say these bottles can take up to 1,000 years to biodegrade.

Drinking water from a reusable stainless steel bottle, like this option from Klean Kanteen, is a healthy choice for both you and the planet. ©Klean Kanteen

If you need any more convincing, consider that oil consumption also comes into play with plastic bottles. The amount of oil required each year for the manufacturing and shipping of bottled water to consumers equals about 1.5 million barrels—enough fuel to power 250,000 homes for one year.

Enter the reusable bottle. A growing awareness of our society's plastic problem has fueled the growth of this eco-conscious item. Today, reusable bottles are available in many sizes, designs, colors, and materials. Since reusable bottles range in cost from about $10 to $20, they are an inexpensive way to go green.

Simply pick one up online or at your local grocer or health food store and fill 'er up. If the tap water in your area is safe and tasty, you can go right to the source. If you prefer filtered water, purchase one of the simple filtration systems (i.e., Brita) for your refrigerator. Reasonably priced systems can also be permanently installed in your kitchen sink.

When choosing a reusable water bottle, veer away from any that show the letters "PC" on the bottom. These contain the much publicized, hormone-disrupting toxin Bisphenol A (BPA), a chemical building block used to make polycarbonate plastic. Better options include stainless steel and clearly marked BPA-free plastic bottles.

In addition to greening your daily H2O, coffee lovers can also help conserve resources by bringing a reusable travel mug to the coffee shop. Many coffee bars will also extend a discount for bringing your own cup.

Two million plastic bottles, most of which end up in landfills, are used in the U.S. every five minutes. ©istockphoto.com/Michael Kemter

4. Tote a Reusable Shopping Bag

ANOTHER SIMPLE WAY to green your daily repertoire is to purchase a few reusable shopping bags and use them instead of the single-use plastic bags supplied by stores today. By using this inexpensive item, you will help preserve natural resources and greatly reduce the amount of trash in our world.

The single-use plastic bags currently flying out the doors in supermarkets and other stores are made of a high-density polyethylene (HDPE). Each year, the world's population uses and then trashes anywhere from 500 billion to one trillion of these plastic bags—this equates to over one million a minute.

The U.S. is responsible for consuming a whopping 380 billion plastic bags, sacks, and wraps a year, according to the EPA. Some estimates peg usage at 552 bags per family per year. In a historic move, in 2007 San Francisco became the first city to ban plastic bags at large supermarkets and chain pharmacies.

Like plastic bottles, these bags are made from petroleum and they are not biodegradable. Instead, they photodegrade in sunlight and, thus, can take up to 1,000 years to break down. They also fill up landfills and pose a threat to the safety of marine and other animal life, which often mistake the bags for food.

If you think a switch to paper bags is a better choice in the checkout line, think again. According to the EPA, 70 percent more global warming gasses are emitted making a paper bag versus a plastic bag, not to mention that precious trees are cut down in the process.

Reusable sacks come in all shapes and sizes, including those that are both eco- and fashion-conscious, like this graphic tote from Envirosax. ©Envirosax

All in all, a reusable sack is your best eco choice. They are available today at most grocery stores, natural foods shops, stores like Wal-Mart and Target, plus a plethora of online retailers. Reusable bags can cost anywhere from a few dollars for utilitarian styles to $10 for more fashionable choices. Materials options range from heavy-duty Cordura nylon and organic cotton to hemp and a fabric made from recycled plastic bottles.

Since most grocery stores now offer bag credits for bringing your own, reusable bags will more than pay for themselves during their lifecycle. For example, if a grocery store offers a 10-cent credit, a $10 bag will completely pay for itself after only 100 uses. Plus, imagine what it will do for your green lifestyle—and your conscience. Toss a few in your car and be sure to bring them along for the ride on every shopping trip. If you get caught without your earth-friendly bag, simply say "no" to the "Paper or plastic?" conundrum and opt for carrying small purchases out of the store in hand.

Opt for a sturdy "green" reusable sack; the world's population uses more than 500 billion plastic bags each year. ©Envirosax

20

5. Buy Green Power

ELECTRIC ENERGY IS WHAT makes today's fast-paced world go 'round. But, did you know that electricity is actually the leading source of greenhouse gas emissions?

Electricity usage is responsible for a full 38 percent of the U.S.'s CO_2 emissions, according to a report from the Pew Center on Global Climate Change. On the flip side, renewable energy sources like wind and solar power, which burn no fossil fuels like natural gas or coal, produce zero emissions. Believe it or not, switching your own home's electricity source to renewable energy can be as simple as making a phone call.

Most homeowners don't have the time or the funds to install an array of solar panels or a wind turbine in their back yard. But, many can still purchase "renewable electricity" directly through their existing utility company (or a competitive power supplier) that delivers clean power sources like wind and solar through the standard utility grid (i.e., power lines, electrical substations, etc.). Contact your local provider to see if they offer this service, which typically has a minimal monthly charge to upgrade your power purchase with blocks of renewable energy.

Wind power is truly clean; it has zero emissions.
©istockphoto.com/Brian Jackson

Even people living in areas where the local utility companies don't offer renewable energy can still get into the game with Renewable Energy Certificates (RECs). Purchasing verified certificates enables you to match up to 100 percent of your electricity usage with clean, renewable energy no matter where you live.

One resource for RECs is 3Degrees (www.3degreesinc.com), which sells these certificates so that anyone can support renewable energy generation. Each REC represents one megawatt-hour (MWh, or 1,000 kilowatt hours) of renewable energy that is generated and delivered to the grid. 3Degrees offers only Green-e certified RECs, which are audited to ensure that only one customer claims credit for each MWh of renewable energy.

Green Idea

A wealth of information on buying Green Power, including a state-by-state guide to renewable energy providers, can be found at the EPA's Green Power website: www.eere.energy.gov/ greenpower.

Conventional energy production can be anything but green. ©istockphoto.com/Bernhard Weber

6. Buy Carbon Offsets

YOU CAN TAKE YOUR commitment to renewable energy one step further by purchasing credits that help offset your own carbon footprint, which is the measure of your environmental impact via your own greenhouse gas (i.e., CO_2) emissions created by activities such as driving, flying, and energy use at home. The purchase of these credits can, in turn, help dissipate the factors causing global warming.

According to Clean Air-Cool Planet, global warming is an "urgent global problem with social, economic, and environmental consequences, resulting from excessive reliance on fossil fuels like coal and oil." It occurs as a result of energy from the sun being trapped by gases (mostly CO_2 and methane) in the atmosphere. These greenhouse gases are a primary result of our society digging up and burning long-buried fossil fuels like coal, natural gas, and oil. Our actions have increased the presence of these gases to the point where the globe is warming and our climate is changing.

Our planet is in need of some assistance. Can you help? ©istockphoto.com/geopaul

We can all do our best to reduce emissions by installing CFLs, choosing to reuse with reusable water bottles and shopping bags, and even minimizing our own carbon footprint with renewable power, but we'll still inevitably use some energy that emits greenhouse gases. This is where carbon offsets come into play. When you buy these credits through reputable organizations, they in turn invest these funds into carbon emissions-reducing projects like building wind power turbines and planting trees. Many of these projects also help build communities by providing jobs.

Look for trusted, verified offset providers like Native Energy (www.nativeeneregy.com) or e-BlueHorizons (www.e-bluehorizons.com). These companies provide convenient CO_2 emissions calculators on their websites so you can add up your own impact for offsetting. Carbon credits range in cost from $36 to offset the yearly emissions of a small car to $96 to offset your home's yearly electricity use. Remember, carbon offsets are meant to supplement your own green efforts, not to replace them. Buying them is an additional contribution that you can make to the planet.

Our use of fossil fuels like oil contribute to greenhouse gas emissions and, thus, global warming.
©istockphoto.com/Wendell Franks

7. Add Organic Food into Your Diet

THERE IS NO QUESTION that a fresh, juicy, organic peach simply tastes better than one that has been grown using pesticides. Still, synthetic pesticides and fertilizers have become a prevalent component in our food system.

Why? In order to meet the world's fast-growing demand for food, producers have had to step up production by using a host of fertilizers and pesticides to ward off crop-devastating insects. But these chemicals are now prolific—an invisible ingredient that poses potential health and environmental hazards.

Organic blueberries are packed with nutrients.
©istockphoto.com/Joe Biafore

According to the Environmental Working Group (EWG), there is growing consensus in the scientific community that small doses of pesticides can adversely affect people, especially pregnant women, developing fetuses, and children, who are more vulnerable to these chemicals.

Research has shown that organically grown foods are higher in cancer-fighting chemicals than conventionally grown foods. In the end, organic farming practices not only yield products that are better for our health, they also focus on farming in ways that minimize the leaching of chemicals into our soils and groundwater.

What Is Organic?

The good news is that, due to consumer demand, the organic foods market is experiencing major growth. Today, about 70 percent of Americans buy organic food occasionally, and nearly one quarter buy it every week, says the Hartman Group, a market research firm.

The U.S. Department of Agriculture (USDA) runs the National Organic Program, which develops and administers national production, handling, and labeling standards for organic agricultural products. Each product must meet USDA standards before being labeled "Organic."

These standards specify that crops must be grown without synthetic pesticides, artificial fertilizers, irradiation (a type of radiation used to kill bacteria), or biotechnology. Animals being raised on organic farms must eat only organically grown feed, not be given synthetic growth hormones or antibiotics, and have access to the outdoors.

Organic foods can be more expensive and many shoppers find it costly to fill up their cart with all organic items. Adding a few organic items to your shopping list will green your cuisine and boost your health quotient.

Look for the USDA Organic stamp on certified organic products. ©USDA

Where Can You Find Organic Foods?

▶ Many chain grocery stores now feature specific organic sections in the produce department and processed foods aisles.

▶ Locate your local natural foods store or co-op. The latter is a cooperative grocery store where shoppers pay a small fee to become "members" who receive discounts on their purchases.

▶ Look for local farmer's markets, which typically run in summer or year-round in warmer climes; many of the farmers here offer organic items.

8. Take a Five-Minute Shower

WHILE WE ALL RELISH the occasional long, steamy shower or hot soak in the tub, it's important to recognize that there is a world water crisis on our planet. In many countries, clean water is extremely hard to come by. More than one billion people in developing countries lack access to a safe supply of drinking water, according to UNICEF. They must walk long distances every day to obtain water for drinking, cooking, and bathing. Additionally, 2.6 billion (40 percent of the earth's population) don't have basic sanitation facilities.

Even though water usually seems plentiful in our own day-to-day lives, many of us don't know just how lucky we are. Think about these facts from Water Partners International (www.water.org), the World Health Organization, and UNICEF:

▶ **Water-related diseases are one of the leading causes of disease and death in the world.**

▶ **More than 5,000 children under the age of five die every day as a result of diarrheal diseases, caused in part by unsafe water.**

▶ **Of all water on earth, 97.5 percent is salt water; of the remaining 2.5 percent fresh water, some 70 percent is frozen in the polar icecaps. The other 30 percent is mostly present as soil moisture or lies in underground aquifers.**

▶ **In the end, less than 1 percent of the world's fresh water (or about 0.007 percent of all water on earth) is readily accessible for direct human use.**

Would you believe that the average American individual uses 100 to 176 gallons of water at home each day? In stark contrast, the average African family uses about 5 gallons of water each day.

A study of student water usage conducted by Princeton University showed the average shower time per day was 12.5 minutes. This equates to more than 40 gallons of water down the drain during each shower.

Water is a precious resource that will continue to dwindle while the earth heats up from global warming. In response, you can green your life simply by doing things like turning the water off while brushing your teeth and shortening your shower time to a no-fuss five minutes. Consider it time well spent for the planet.

Water is one of the planet's most precious resources. Are you letting it go down the drain?
©istockphoto.com/Kiyoshi Takahase

9. Unplug at Home

Since our electricity habits are obviously contributing greatly to our share of the planet's greenhouse gas emissions, it just makes good sense to do things like turn off lights when leaving a room and power off appliances when they're not in use. As a bonus, this green step will also help whittle down your energy bills.

The EPA estimates that household electronics, many of which use energy for displays even when turned "off," account for almost 5 percent of a home's energy bills. For example, running a computer and its monitor 24 hours a day can use up to 1,100 kilowatt hours annually. Putting these items, from computers to stereos, on sleep mode could save more than 80 percent of that expense and cut CO_2 emissions by up to 1,250 pounds a year.

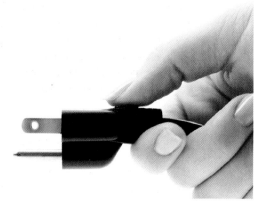

Going out? Powering down or unplugging appliances will save untold amounts of energy.
©istockphoto.com/ranplett

What to Power Down

▶ **Unplug seldom-used appliances:** Got a fridge in the garage that's cooling just a few sodas? Transfer your drinks to the main fridge and unplug its garage counterpart. You could even save up to $10 a month on your utility bill.

▶ **Unplug chargers:** No doubt, you have an array of plastic power chargers to keep your cell phones, PDAs, and digital cameras up and running. If they're plugged in, they're using power. Keep them unplugged until you need them.

▶ **Turn off the tube:** Even at rest (i.e., turned off), your TVs, DVD players, VCRs, and stereos are sucking energy. All together, their "standby" consumption can be equal to that of a 100-watt light bulb running continuously. One quick way to turn them all off when you're leaving the house is to connect them to a single power strip.

▶ **Set computers to sleep:** Enabling the "sleep mode" feature for periods of inactivity on your computer can make a huge difference in its energy consumption. In Windows, the power management settings are found on your computer's Control Panel. Mac users can look for energy saving settings under "System Preferences" in the Apple menu.

—Information courtesy NRDC

10. Plant a Tree

TREES GIVE SHADE ON hot days and shelter from rainstorms, plus they offer themselves up time and time again for our daily needs. From office paper to wood-frame homes, the tree is a pillar of our society.

Our deeply rooted friends also happen to remove carbon dioxide from the atmosphere and store it within their own plant material and the surrounding soil. Carbon is a gas that trees use to grow and reproduce during photosynthesis. Given today's greenhouse gas troubles, the tree population is certainly working overtime.

Plant it. An average tree is believed to absorb one ton of carbon dioxide over its normal lifetime.
©istockphoto.com/Amanda Rohde

The amount of carbon dioxide a tree can store varies widely. A 30-year-old, fast-growing hard-wood tree like a red mulberry or laurel oak will soak up an average of 69.5 pounds of CO_2 per year. The bigger the tree, the more carbon it can sequester. Those with large trunk diameters and dense wood are the best trees for the job, says the U.S. Forest Service. Leafed trees also work harder than conifers.

Since larger hardwood trees often grow much slower in colder, northern climates, some experts believe that trees planted in equatorial rainforests are more effective at battling the global warming trend.

According to the Eco Preservation Society, if every American family planted just one tree, CO_2 in the atmosphere would be reduced by one billion pounds annually. That's nearly 5 percent of the amount the earth's population pumps into the atmosphere each year.

While it seems all the things we do, places we go, and items we consume require energy and create climate-changing emissions, planting a tree is a reversal of this tide. A signal of change. Go ahead and get your hands dirty.

Quick and easy ways to plant a tree:

• **The Arbor Day Foundation (www.arborday.org) enables you to give the gift of trees through its Give-a-Tree Greeting card program. For $5.95, you can send a card that honors the occasion with a tree planted in a national forest that has been devastated by insects, disease, or wildfires.**

• **The Nature Conservancy has launched the Plant a Billion campaign (www.plantabillion. org) to literally plant a billion trees in an effort to bring back the tropical Atlantic Forest in Brazil and, ultimately, help combat climate change. Each tree costs $1.**

• **If time is on your side and you'd like to plant your own tree, check out www.treepeople.org for detailed information on the process.**

Week One: Green Your Home

THE ONE PLACE YOU CAN MAKE THE MOST difference to the environment and your family's health is in your own home. On average, most Americans spend at least 14 hours a day in their abode, much of which is focused on household chores and activities that consume a significant amount of energy and water.

The typical U.S. household consumes about 11,000 kilowatt-hours (kWh) each year, which rings up an average annual electricity bill of $900, according to the U.S. Department of Energy. This equates to an average "carbon footprint" for a U.S. household of 19 metric tons of CO_2. It is apparent that our consumption habits at home are why changes made there have such a significant impact.

But, reducing energy use at home is just the beginning of greening your lifestyle. A focus on reducing water use as well as cleaning up indoor air quality are key to sustaining health and happiness.

This first week will focus on relatively simple and mostly inexpensive changes you can make at home on all these fronts. Congratulations. You are officially on the road to going green. And so your earth-friendly journey begins—at home.

The Air We Breathe

WHILE HOME IS WHERE THE heart is, it can also be one of the most toxic places on the planet. Would you believe the Environmental Protection Agency (EPA) reports that most homes have airborne concentrations of organic pollutants that are at least two to five times higher than the air outside?

According to the World Health Organization, indoor air pollution ranks among the top five environmental risks to public health. This is a serious problem, especially when you consider that Americans spend 90 percent of their time indoors. Some homes are subject to effects from unique toxins like asbestos, radon, and formaldehyde, but the majority of poor indoor air quality is caused by the ingredients present in common household cleaning products.

Many conventional cleaning products contain harmful VOCs. ©istockphoto.com/Floortje

While many of these products get the job done to deliver a clean, sparkling home, they are anything but healthy. In fact, they are harboring a dirty secret called volatile organic compounds (VOCs), a type of irritating chemical found in many conventional products that can evaporate or off-gas into your home's air supply. In the short term, VOCs can cause symptoms like headaches, nausea, visual impairment, and memory loss. Their long-term effects are even more severe—hormone disruption, liver and kidney damage, and possibly cancer.

In addition to seeping into your indoor air supply, these common chemicals can also be bad for the planet. According to the Clean Water Fund, more than 32 million pounds of household cleaning products are poured down the drain each year nationwide, heading into sewage treatment plants. Many of these products, including dishwashing and laundry detergents, break down into environmental estrogens that can slip through water processing plants and into our soil and water sources. As a result, these cancer-causing estrogens, which are synthetic substances that can disrupt hormonal balance and metabolism function when absorbed into a person's system, can negatively affect the health of both wildlife and humans.

Clean Up Your Act

Holding your breath yet? Fear not—a growing number of natural, green cleaning options and products on the market today can help you transition your home into a toxin-free zone. You can also speed up the process by opening windows regularly to ventilate your home. Adding a houseplant or two into your décor will also soak up airborne chemicals like formaldehyde and benzene. The best air-purifying choices include the Boston fern, Areca palm, and rubber plant.

Eco Facts

Living in a Chemical World

- **Studies show that women who work in the home have a 55 percent higher risk of developing cancer and/or chronic respiratory disease than those working outside the home.**

- **A study focusing on work-related asthma in four states conducted by Michigan State University found that 12 percent of all cases were associated with exposure to cleaning products.**

- **According to the EPA, household cleaners also contribute to smog formation. By 2020, household product emissions are projected to surpass tailpipe emissions to become Los Angeles' Number One cause of smog.**

Cost Meter: $

Many Americans are making the move to purify their air quality and boost their health quotient. According to a 2008 study by Mintel, a leading market research company, sales of green/natural household cleaners (including pet care and paper products) rose by almost 30 percent from $409 million in 2004 to $528 million in 2006.

Today, consumer demand has many companies touting products that are "natural," "organic," or "eco-friendly," but not all of these are actually good for you or the planet. Because cleaning supply companies classify their chemical brews as "trade secrets," they are only required to divulge the most offensive toxins on their labels (typically only 1 percent of the total). This fact means that most are under no legal or regulatory obligation to be concerned about how their products might harm our health.

Be wary of "greenwashing" and start reading the labels of those cleaning products you aim to buy. The first step is to keep any hazardous product that says "Danger" or "Poison" on the label out of your home. Additionally, anything that is marked with a "Warning" or "Caution" label is another to be avoided.

Green Idea

The best way to get rid of your unwanted and unnatural cleaning products is to simply finish using them or, if you're anxious about their chemical content, take them to a household hazardous waste center for disposal. Whatever you do, don't dump them down the drain and into the world's water supply.

Aim for products labeled with specific terms like "plant-based," "solvent-free," or "no phosphates." You can also look for brands that choose to reveal their list of ingredients. Many of these products are made from natural, biodegradable, plant-based ingredients that you can feel comfortable using. Two companies that have put the onus on what's inside their products are Seventh Generation and Ecover, both of which are available in most health food stores and many major supermarket chains.

Green up your act by swapping your toxin-infused conventional cleaners—from laundry and dishwasher detergent to glass and toilet cleaner—for natural options, many of which perform equally as well. This can be done slowly or in one fell swoop. Green cleaners tend to cost just a little more, but, in the end, you are making a wise investment in your health.

Beeswax candles are a healthier, natural option to traditional air fresheners.
©Bluecorn Naturals

Green on the Cheap

A 1999 University of Bristol study revealed that frequent use of air fresheners and aerosol sprays in the home contributed to 25 percent more headaches and 19 percent more incidences of depression in new mothers, plus 30 percent more ear infections in infants. Ditch your aerosol air fresheners and plug-ins for soy or beeswax candles infused with essential oils, a natural, clean-burning option that provides a fresh fragrance to your home. Long-lasting, 18-hour pillar candles can cost as little as $9 from beeswaxcandles.com. You can also make your own air freshener by combining five to ten drops of an essential oil like lavender, lemon, or sweet orange with two cups of water in a spray bottle.

Making Your Own Green Cleaners

ONE OF THE EASIEST, most inexpensive ways to make your home a healthier, more earth-friendly place is to concoct your own cleaners from simple, toxin-free ingredients. These are things you probably already have in your kitchen—baking soda, vinegar, lemon juice, vegetable oil. If you would prefer to avoid the slightly extra expense of buying green cleaning products, then mixing up your own might be the way to go. These natural concoctions will save you money, even over the unhealthy cleaning product options available in the store. Now, that's good green sense.

The following homemade cleaning alternatives, recommended by the EPA, will fill your needs for many cleaning duties. You'll need measuring spoons and cups, plus a few clean, reusable containers or spray bottles.

Cost Meter:

- ▶ **Glass cleaner:** The average glass cleaner contains butyl cellusolve, which can damage liver, kidneys, and red blood cells. Natural Replacement: Mix one tablespoon of white vinegar or lemon juice in one quart of water; spray on surfaces to be cleaned and wipe off as normal.

- ▶ **Furniture polish:** A common ingredient in most furniture polish is petroleum distillates, which can cause nerve damage and skin and eye irritation. Natural Replacement: Mix one teaspoon of lemon juice in one pint of mineral or vegetable oil; spray on wood furniture/ surfaces and wipe off.

- ▶ **Toilet bowl cleaner:** Most conventional toilet cleaners contain corrosive ingredients that can cause severe skin, eye, and respiratory irritation, including asthma attacks. Natural Replacement: Toss some baking soda or vinegar into the bowl and scrub with a toilet brush. Note: You can also make a paste of baking soda and water to scrub up tubs, sinks, and counters.

- ▶ **Oven cleaner:** Found in many oven cleaners, sodium hydroxide, otherwise known as lye, delivers extreme irritation to eyes, nose, and throat; it can also burn tissue upon contact. Natural Replacement: Lose the lye in your home by cleaning spills with steel wool and baking soda as soon as the oven cools; for tough stains, add salt (avoid the salt, however, if you have a self-cleaning or continuous-cleaning oven).

- ▶ **Drain cleaner:** This product also contains dangerous sodium hydroxide. Natural Replacement: Keep hair and debris out of sinks with an inexpensive sink screen; if duty calls, use a plumber's snake or plunger to clear the drain.

Waste Not: The Problem with Trash

D O YOU KNOW where your trash goes? It's pretty easy to forget about it once it's gone, but after our trash is picked up by the garbage truck, it gets tossed into a landfill or an incinerator. In the U.S., about 26 percent of our waste is recycled or composted and 8 percent is burned at incinerators. The rest—a whopping 66 percent—is piled high into landfills across the country. When you consider that the average American produces almost 4.5 pounds of trash each day (compared with an average of about 2.7 in 1960), you can begin to visualize how the tons of trash start to add up across the country.

While landfills are the oldest form of mass waste disposal in the U.S., they are also the second-largest human-related source of methane emissions, a potent greenhouse gas. In 2006, landfills accounted for almost 23 percent of all methane emissions. This landfill gas (LFG) is born as the solid waste decomposes under anaerobic conditions (sans oxygen).

Green Idea

Some initial efforts are underway to capture Landfill Gas (LFG), which can actually be converted and used as an energy source. This act helps prevent methane from making its way into the atmosphere and tacking an extra burden onto local smog and climate change problems. Methane can be used to generate electricity or to replace fossil fuels for industrial use, or it can be converted into pipeline-quality gas. In Pennsylvania, UGI Utilities, Inc., the state's largest natural gas and electric utility, recently broke ground on a nine-mile pipeline to transport converted LFG to four industrial companies in the Lancaster County area. It is believed this local production will conserve 10,000 barrels of oil each year.

The U.S. has almost 4,000 active landfills and over 10,000 old municipal landfills, according to the EPA.
©istockphoto.com/Jacom Stephens

In addition to the problems associated with our overflowing landfills, some trash inevitably lands in wild and natural places like the ocean or our waterways, where it can break down and harm wildlife and even people. You can help reduce the world's overabundance of trash by choosing to reduce, reuse, and recycle. These three effective "Rs" are extremely simple and purely cost-free. At the end of the day, you may actually end up saving money.

Waste Not: Reduce, Reuse, Recycle

BEING CONSCIOUS OF THE three Rs at home and elsewhere will help you realize your quest to go green. Implement just a few of the ideas from these conservation concepts this week, but try to continue to make this mantra a part of your life going forward.

Reduce

The first "R" refers to limiting the amount of things you buy or use in your daily life. Instead of grabbing a handful of paper towels to wipe up a spill, can you use half the amount or a cloth instead? This simple act can help lessen the burden on our trash system. Can you bring your lunch to work in reusable containers instead of getting takeout and tossing the packaging? By packing your cuisine in reusable containers instead of plastic wrap or bags, you can also help reduce the amount of waste you produce. You can also avoid a great deal of packaging by buying food from the bulk bins that are a fixture in most health food stores. Here, you can fill up your own reusable containers with everything from rice and pasta to dried fruit and candy. Just be sure to have your empty container weighed in at the checkout before filling it up. In addition, buying only the groceries you need each week will also help limit the amount of spoiled food you end up tossing.

Cost Meter: $0
(these changes will save you money)

Reuse

Studies show that between 2 and 5 percent of the waste stream is potentially reusable. Reusing the things that you can will help prevent tons of trash from making their way into landfills.

A great example of a reusable item that can make a difference is rechargeable batteries. Each year, over 15 billion batteries are sold worldwide, most of which are thrown away after a single use. Invest in some quality reusable batteries and a slow-charging charger that will best maintain their lifespan; within a year, this investment will more than likely have paid for itself. [**Note:** All batteries contain some amount of mercury and should, thus, be recycled by an authorized location. Check www.Earth911.org for locations near you.]

Another productive switch you can make is to bring your own reusable shopping bags when you hit the supermarket to reduce the unnecessary disposal of plastic and paper shopping bags.

These bags, available in fabrics from eco-friendly hemp to organic cotton, are inexpensive and easy to use; just remember to keep a stock in your car so you're not caught in the checkout line being asked "Paper or plastic?"

You will also make a major impact and up your green quotient exponentially if you choose to drink from a reusable bottle instead of throwing countless single-use bottles into the trash. Best bets for your health include BPA-free plastic bottles (avoid "PC" or recycling number 7, stamped on the bottom) and stainless steel versions.

Recycle

This simple act is one of the best things you can do for the planet. Many towns today have a curbside recycling program; in fact, www.Earth911.org says that over 85 percent of Americans have access to local recycling programs. Contact your city office for information on getting set up with the service and the appropriate containers. Then, simply sort your recyclables like glass, aluminum, and paper into the separate bins for pickup. Those without a local service are likely to have a recycling center in the vicinity where these items can be dropped off. Some centers will even pay for your more valuable recyclables.

A 2007 Harris Poll showed that one-quarter of Americans still recycle nothing at all.
©istockphoto.com/Bruce Lonngren

Becoming Paper Savvy

OMPLETE THE CIRCLE and catch the flip side of recycling by adding recycled paper products like toilet paper, paper towels, and tissues into your repertoire. Today, according to the National Resources Defense Council (NRDC), Americans use a whopping 741 pounds of paper products each year per person—this is more than double the per capita consumption in 1960. We also consume more than any other country in the world. But, paper is difficult to avoid. From our mail and magazines to catalogs and cardboard, it is an ubiquitous part of our lives.

A plethora of problems exist with paper. First and foremost is that much of the production today cuts down trees, which are important heroes in fighting climate change. Each tree that is cut down would have absorbed one ton of carbon dioxide or more over its normal lifetime. Cutting trees down also triggers the release of CO_2 from denuded soils. Some experts suggest that deforestation and the resulting land degradation could be responsible for up to 20 percent of all greenhouse gases created by human activity. Additionally, any paper that is not recycled generally floats into landfills, further exacerbating the world's trash problems.

The good news is that Americans recycle more than half of all the paper they use each year. This waste, along with scrap wood from lumber mills, makes up about half of all materials used today to produce paper. Still, there are many "virgin" paper products on the market that use little to no post-consumer (i.e., recycled) fibers in their manufacture. These are good ones to avoid if you're on the path to going green.

Choosing recycled paper products will greatly reduce the need to cut down more trees.
©istockphoto.com/Klaus Hollitzer

Using Recycled Paper Products

WHEN DOING YOUR weekly grocery shopping, look for paper products that report their content percentages of recycled and/or post-consumer fibers right on the package. Post-consumer fibers are sourced from paper that was previously used and would otherwise have made its way into a landfill or an incinerator. These types of earth-friendly products are readily available at local health food stores and most major supermarket chains.

Cost Meter:

Your eco-consciousness will help save an impressive amount of precious trees. According to the NRDC, if every household in the U.S. replaced just one box of virgin fiber facial tissues (175 sheets) with 100 percent recycled tissue, we could save 163,000 trees. The same action undertaken with one roll of virgin fiber toilet paper (500 sheets) would save 423,900 trees. Napkins raise the bar even more. Replacing a 250-count package of virgin fiber napkins with 100 percent recycled serviettes would save a whopping one million trees. You get the picture.

Eco Facts

- Most of the world's paper supply is sourced from timber logged in regions with biologically diverse and ecologically valuable habitat.

- The Southern U.S., which is the largest paper-producing region in the world, logs an estimated 5 million acres of forests (an area the size of New Jersey) each year.

- The trees for most of the world's paper supply, about 85 percent, are sourced from forests. Only 15 percent are harvested from tree farms.

- According to the Organization for Economic Cooperation and Development, the pulp and paper industry is the third-greatest industrial greenhouse gas emitter. Its carbon dioxide emissions are expected to double by 2020.

- Paper is white, not brown like trees, because it is whitened using chemicals like chlorine bleach, chlorine dioxide, or hydrogen peroxide. This process can produce cancer-causing chemicals such as dioxins and furans.

The most abundant options for household paper products are those with zero recycled or post-consumer content. Check your packages carefully and look for markings that indicate the product you are considering buying is actually made with recycled content, and especially post-consumer fibers. Check out http://www.nrdc.org/land/forests/gtissue.asp for a comprehensive shopping guide to home tissue products.

Interestingly, according to the EPA, paper cannot be recycled indefinitely. In fact, papermaking fibers can typically be recycled five to seven times before they become too short and weak to be recycled again. For this reason, it is still necessary for the paper industry to harvest some new fiber (i.e., from trees) that can be infused into the recycled paper manufacturing process.

Green on the Cheap

Help save the planet and stop your junk mail at the same time by signing up with www.GreenDimes.com. This free service halts up to 90 percent of your junk mail by working with you and the country's largest group of marketers and catalogs to pinpoint and eliminate the mail you don't want to receive. To date, Green Dimes has worked with over 300,000 people to stop the unnecessary delivery of almost 2.5 million catalogs and 13,000 pounds of junk mail. Basic service is free; upgrading to the $20 premium service makes the process more streamlined, allows you to remove unlimited household names from junk mail lists, and plants five trees. So far, GreenDimes has planted over one million trees.

Each ton of 100% post-consumer recycled fiber that replaces a ton of virgin fiber saves between 12 and 24 trees. ©istockphoto.com/AVTG

Becoming Water Conscious

DURING THE 20TH CENTURY, the world's population tripled. But in this time, our water usage (of renewable resources) actually increased by six times, according to the World Water Council. Will our demand continue to outpace our supply? Factor in the reality that the population is slated to increase another 40 to 50 percent in the next 50 years, and you can imagine how resources will continue to be taxed.

Today, many countries, including the U.S., are struggling with drought conditions that will likely worsen as climate change's effects are realized. In Chapter 2 of this book, it was reported that less than 1 percent of the world's fresh water (or about 0.007 percent of all water on earth) is readily accessible for direct human use. A finite supply coupled with increasing demand has put the world in the midst of a water crisis. According to the EPA, a recent government survey showed at least 36 U.S. states are anticipating local, regional, or statewide water shortages by 2013.

The EPA says that if all U.S. households installed water-efficient appliances, the country would save more than three trillion gallons of water and more than $18 billion per year. ©istockphoto.com/Florea Marius

Eco Fact

The biggest offender in household water use is our toilet, which sucks down 18 gallons per person each day and accounts for over 26 percent of total daily use. Other culprits include showers and faucets, which together send a full 43 percent of our water resources down the drain.

Green Idea

If one out of every 100 American homes were retrofitted with water-efficient fixtures like low-flow shower-heads, we could save about 100 million kWh of electricity per year and avoid 80,000 tons of greenhouse gas emissions. That is equivalent to removing nearly 15,000 automobiles from the road for one year.

As you can see, conserving water is an elemental part of going green, but it can also help you save money. The average American household uses approximately 350 gallons of water each day; that's almost 128,000 gallons a year. The EPA reports that the average household incurs a yearly water bill of $500. It also suggests that simple changes made to use water efficiently could save you about $170 each year.

You can actually reduce your own personal water use by over 45 gallons a day simply by installing more efficient water fixtures, such as low-flow faucet and showerhead aerators, and checking for leaks on a regular basis. That adds up to 1,350 gallons per month and a whole lot of money saved. Also, look for the EPA's WaterSense label on products like bathroom faucets when you're in the market for a new fixture; this denotes an item that helps conserve water. You can make a difference by limiting the amount of water you use every day.

Installing low-flow faucet and shower aerators is one of the simplest ways to conserve water. ©istockphoto.com/David Mingay

Conserving Water

NOW THAT YOU UNDERSTAND why reducing our water use benefits the environment and our bottom lines, hopefully you are inspired to make some changes. These constructive, cost-efficient ideas will help you green your daily household water use:

▶ **Turning it off:** Most bathroom faucets flow at a rate of two gallons per minute, which is a lot of water down the drain if it's running while you're shaving or brushing your teeth. Shutting off the spigot while you brush your teeth can save up to an impressive eight gallons of water per day.

▶ **Showering shorter:** A 2001 study conducted by Moen Plumbing Supply revealed that the average American spends about eight minutes in the shower. Shaving off a few minutes can save a ton of water—a five-minute shower uses about 10 to 25 gallons. On the flip side, a full bathtub requires about 70 gallons of water.

▶ **Fixing leaks:** If it drips at a rate of one drop per second, a leaky faucet can waste more than 3,000 gallons of water yearly. A leaky toilet can waste up to 200 gallons each and every day of the year. Tighten these water-wasters up and you'll make a huge difference to our water supply. You can also check for hidden water leaks by monitoring the house water meter before and after a two-hour period when no water is being used. If there is a leak, it might be time to call the plumber.

Cost Meter: $0
(this change will save you money)

▶ **Loading it up:** The average washing machine uses about 41 gallons of water for each load of laundry. To conserve water with this chore, wash only full loads or use the appropriate load size selection setting on your washing machine.

▶ **Tricking the system:** You can greatly reduce the amount of water your toilet uses by putting plastic bottles or a float booster in your toilet tank. For a cheap resolve, put an inch or two of sand or pebbles inside two plastic bottles, fill them with water, and place them in the tank safely away from the operating mechanisms. To ensure it continues to flush properly, make sure at least three gallons stay in the tank. This fix could save up to ten or more gallons of water per day.

Greening Your Home Office

IN 2004, OVER 20 MILLION people worked at home, according to the U.S. Department of Labor's Bureau of Labor Statistics. Are you one of this number, which represents more than 15 percent of all workers over age 16? Whether you are lucky enough to work at home or simply have a space in the house for catching up on e-mails and bills, you can also easily make your home office more environmentally friendly.

First off, if you are telecommuting, you're already there. On average, workers spend more than 100 gas-guzzling hours commuting to work each year. A small percentage of these people are on public transit; the rest are driving cars, which contribute greatly to climate-changing carbon emissions.

Cost Meter: **$**

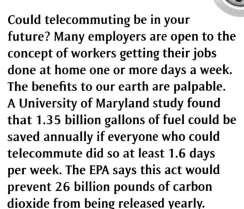

Green Idea

Could telecommuting be in your future? Many employers are open to the concept of workers getting their jobs done at home one or more days a week. The benefits to our earth are palpable. A University of Maryland study found that 1.35 billion gallons of fuel could be saved annually if everyone who could telecommute did so at least 1.6 days per week. The EPA says this act would prevent 26 billion pounds of carbon dioxide from being released yearly.

Don't have a home office? Ask your employer if they are willing to implement a few green ideas like recycling and using recycled paper.
©istockphoto.com/Konstantin Inozemtsev

IMPLEMENTING THESE HOME OFFICE TIPS will help you complete the circle and wrap up your first week of green changes. Kudos to you for greening your home.

1. **Reducing paper use:** Try to avoid using the printer and photocopier as much as possible. Do you really need to print out that report? Perhaps you can share it via e-mail or on a CD-ROM instead. If you do need to perform these tasks, try to print or copy on both sides of the paper you are using. In addition, instead of printing out receipts or documents, save the file on your computer. Just be sure to regularly back up your valuable information to an external disk.

2. **Buying recycled products:** Whether it's printer paper or office furniture, try to seek out options that are recycled. Most office supply stores offer an excellent array of recycled paper options that include post-consumer waste. One resource recommended by the EPA for green office supplies is www.greenearthofficesupplies.com.

3. **Recycling in the office:** Make sure to stow an extra trash can for recycling under your desk to toss that used paper right into. This can be emptied in your home's paper recycling bin on collection day or taken to your local recycling center.

4. **Pack it with shredding:** If you're like many Americans, you shred your financial or personal documents instead of tossing them in the recycling bin. But, shredded paper can also have a second life—use it as protective padding when shipping boxes and replace the need for bubble wrap or packing "peanuts."

5. **Host it green:** If you have a website for your business or even for family photos and information, make it eco-conscious by choosing a green web hosting company, such as www.gogreenhosting.com, which offsets 100 percent of its energy use with certified wind power.

6. **Conferencing instead of commuting:** Need to meet with a client or co-worker? Save yourself the trouble and expense of travel and nip those substantial carbon emissions in the bud by choosing instead to host a conference call or video conference.

Green Review:
Changes to Focus on During Week One

1. When buying cleaning products read the labels to try to determine if harmful ingredients are present. Or, opt only for products from companies that choose to reveal their full ingredient list.

2. As you finish them, replace your harmful home cleaning products with more natural versions that will help clean up your indoor air quality and keep related health problems at bay.

3. Concoct a few of your own green cleaners at home with simple ingredients you probably already have stocked in your kitchen.

4. Try to follow the simple philosophy of the three Rs, by reducing, reusing, and recycling. Even if you accomplish one act in each area, you will have made a difference.

5. When it's time to replace a household paper product like toilet paper or paper towels, take a recycled product, preferably one from 100-percent post-consumer waste, for a test run.

6. Conserve water by employing H_2O-saving tactics such as turning off the bathroom faucet while you shave or brush your teeth and fine-tuning your shower time to a reasonable five minutes.

7. Green your home office by choosing green strategies like reducing paper use, choosing recycled paper products, and organizing meetings via phone if possible.

©istockphoto.com/DivaNir4a

TrueGreen: More Smart Ideas for the Home

T HE SUGGESTIONS ON THIS page and the next few (TrueGreen and SuperGreen) are purely extra credit. They tend to be more expensive and/or time-consuming, earth-friendly concepts. If you're inspired, make these changes when it's right for you. Or, file them for future consideration.

Buying Green Linens

There are many excellent reasons to spend your dollars on green products when purchasing items for the home. Take your shower curtain and liner, for instance. That olfactory experience (i.e., "new product smell") present when you hang a new curtain up for use is actually the product's release of toxic chemicals; this is called "off-gassing."

A recent study conducted by the Center for Health, Environment & Justice (CHEJ), a non-profit organization focused on preventing environmental health harms caused by chemical threats, found that shower curtains made with polyvinyl chloride (PVC) plastic contain a host of harmful chemicals, including VOCs and phthalates. It showed that new shower curtains released 108 different VOCs into the air over 28 days. For the first seven days, these toxic chemicals permeated the air and measured in at over 16 times greater than the recommended guidelines for indoor air quality established by the U.S. Green Building Council.

Earth-friendly linens just might make you sleep better at night. ©istockphoto.com/Baloncici

Green Idea

Today, many chain stores, including Wal-Mart, are offering a selection of linens that feature organic and sustainably farmed materials. In addition, a number of online retailers have cropped up to serve consumers' eco-conscious desires. Here are a few options:

- **www.goodnightnaturals.com**

- **www.looporganic.com**

- **www.bambooandorganiclinens.com**

- **www.annasova.com**

When you're in the market for a new shower curtain and liner, steer clear of PVC and look for healthier, more eco-conscious fabric options like bamboo, hemp, or organic cotton. These sustainable fabrics are also stellar choices for all your other home linens, from bedding and towels to dish cloths and placemats.

For example, organic cotton is grown with methods that have a low impact on the environment and consumers, namely because its production uses no toxic pesticides and fertilizers. More than 2.3 billion pounds of fertilizers are employed on U.S. farms each year. Conversely, much of today's organic cotton is actually grown in the U.S.; the Organic Trade Association reports that in 2004, farmers in four states harvested over three million pounds.

Bamboo, which reaches its maturity in a few months, is a truly sustainable resource. It also has anti-bacterial and deodorizing properties that make it a great material for towels, bedding, and shower curtains.

By buying sustainably produced linens, you are supporting the kind of farming that respects our environment. It can be a slightly more expensive purchase than conventional linens, but you can rest easy knowing you are also keeping the chemicals that can be released from PVC and fabrics produced with fertilizers to a minimum in your home.

SuperGreen: More Big Ideas for the Home

MOTIVATED TO DO EVEN MORE? Going SuperGreen takes time and commitment, but it can also be purely simple if you are making big changes or purchases anyway. At the very least, it is solid food for thought.

Eco-conscious Renovating

Are you planning to paint a room, redo your kitchen, or even build a new home? If going green is at the forefront of your day-to-day life, then this is a perfect time to put your mantra into action in a bigger way. According to the American Institute of Architects, the number of cities with green building programs (i.e., providing tax credits and community planning) has increased more than 400 percent since 2003.

A study by McGraw-Hill Construction and the U.S. Green Building Council also found that going green was the top reason for home renovations completed by respondents. Because of the push in green building in the last few years, we are lucky to live in a time when there is an ever-increasing array of eco-friendly options for home improvement.

There is so much information on this topic that entire books, websites, and blogs have been written on the subject. We'll just touch the surface here but still attempt to get your wheels turning with some key ideas and resources.

▶ **Painting a room?** Choose green paints like those from Bioshield that are non-toxic and environmentally friendly and that come in low- and no-VOC versions. Many companies offer a wide variety of colors plus primers, stains, and sealers.

▶ **Buying new appliances?** Hone in on the choices that are ENERGY STAR® qualified. These appliances have been built to use less energy than other products, which saves you money on utility bills, helps conserve resources, and protects the environment, all at the same time. The ENERGY STAR label can be found on everything from household appliances and home electronics to windows and light fixtures. In addition, water-saving faucets and low-flow toilets will also serve you and the environment well.

▶ **Re-roofing or re-shingling?** This is a perfect time to consider installing a few solar panels on top of your home. With the renewed tax credits for solar still available, this energy-producing endeavor will surely pay for itself within a few years. Recycled roofing options also exist.

▶ **Shopping for new furniture?** Whether you're in the market for a new sofa or a dining table, there are also eco options for all furniture needs. Used or antique furniture is earth-friendly because by purchasing it you are reducing the need for more production and energy expended—you could also be saving more trash from heading to a landfill. Recycled furniture has also gained popularity in the last few years, along with Forest Stewardship Council (FSC) certified wood furniture. Companies like The Simple Furniture Company, which produces the Inmodern collection, meet FSC standards for environmentally responsible forestry.

A change of hue can be good for the body and soul, especially if it's done with eco-paints. ©Tomas Bercic

Eco Fact

If you are remodeling your home, consider that if it was built before 1960, it likely contains heavily leaded paints, the exposure to which can have severe effects on young children and the unborn children of pregnant women. Houses built before 1978 may also contain leaded paints, according to the EPA. This old paint is the most significant source of lead exposure in the U.S. today, so care should be taken when remodeling because dust from these paints could put you and your family at risk. For more information, check out http://www.epa.gov/iaq/homes/hip-lead.html.

▶ **Putting in new carpet or flooring?** Conventionally produced carpeting has been shown to off-gas VOCs. Wool carpeting is a natural, biodegradable, ultra-low toxicity floor covering choice; Nature's Carpet is one brand that is Carpet and Rug Institute Green Label Plus certified. Durable cork and elegant bamboo flooring are also eco-conscious choices.

▶ **Building a home or addition?** Green building materials like straw bales and RASTRA block (made from recycled foam plastics) make it easy for you to create an entirely green abode. This is a perfect time to implement eco-friendly, energy-saving systems like passive solar, on-demand hot water heating, or geothermal heating. For more information on green building, check out www.greenhomeguide.org.

ore earth-frie

Week Two:
Green Your Energy

WHERE WOULD WE BE WITHOUT ENERGY? It heats our homes, cooks our food, and delivers entertainment via our televisions and computers. Its sources are varied—coal, natural gas, oil, nuclear, renewable energies—and its demand increases every single day as the world's population grows.

Of all the energy consumed by Americans, almost 40 percent is allotted to generating electricity, most of which is produced with fossil fuels. But, as the planet's fossil fuel reserves dwindle, our demand is likely to soon outpace our supply.

The use of fossil fuels also contributes greatly to our growing problem with climate-changing CO_2 in the atmosphere. In fact, residential energy consumption accounts for over 20 percent of all carbon emissions and energy use. Some view the answer in increasing our use of renewable energies like solar, wind, and hydroelectric, but these clean technologies still only account for less than 7 percent of our energy supply. Others think the answer lies in amping up around the world with a plethora of nuclear power plants. What would you like our energy landscape to look like in 10, 20, or 50 years?

Today, you can help reduce the burden on the planet—and our dependence on watts—by taking a few simple, low-cost measures to step back your own household's energy consumption. This week, your green charge is all about power.

The History of Energy

THE U.S. HAS had a long and intensifying relationship with energy. In 1776, when the U.S. declared its independence from Great Britain, nearly all energy was still produced from pure muscle power and fuelwood. Our vast supply of coal and petroleum still lay in waiting.

During the early 19th century, coal began to catch on, as did natural gas (as an illuminant) and electricity. At the close of World War I, coal accounted for 75 percent of the country's energy production. As America industrialized, its appetite for energy became voracious, quadrupling between 1880 and 1918. The immense supply of coal fed the fever, but petroleum spilled onto the energy landscape with the discovery of an enormous Texas oil field in 1901. The timing was right as it practically coincided with the launch of the Ford Model T, regarded as the first affordable car, and the advent of mass-produced automobiles.

About 600 coal plants operate in the U.S. today.
©istockphoto.com/Rob Belknap

After World War II, coal lost ground to petrol as trucks that ran on gasoline and diesel fuel overtook trains as a method of transporting goods. Natural gas found a new market with home heating, replacing the coal that had been used in many home furnaces and ranges. What would become of coal? It would live on as an energy source that would be utilized to fuel the electrification of the country.

New energy sources like nuclear power began to emerge later in the 20th century and other older sources like hydroelectric and geothermal gained renewed interest as the country's energy needs increased. Today, most energy in the U.S., along with the rest of the industrialized world, is produced using fossil fuels, including coal, natural gas, and crude oil.

Over 40,000 oil fields are located around the globe, including those on land and offshore.
©istockphoto.com/Alan Tobey

How We Use Energy

O N OUR BIG, BLUE PLANET, North America is by far the largest consumer of energy. In fact, the U.S. alone demands a full 22 percent of the world's energy. Looking back through history, the United States was able to supply the lion's share of its energy needs, save for short periods during Colonial times when coal was imported from Great Britain.

Americans stepped things up in the '60s, however, and our needs quickly outran U.S. production in the coming decades. By 2000, the U.S. was only able to generate 73 percent of its own energy needs, making our country dependent on imports of nearly 29 quadrillion Btu (British thermal units).

Not surprisingly, the energy consumption of the world—and the U.S.—is only expected to grow. But just how much it is slated to increase is impressive. A recent report from the U.S. Energy Information Agency projects that it will increase by 50 percent from 2005 to 2030.

The fast-developing economies and growing populations of China and India will drive much of the global growth, raising their share of the world's total energy consumption from 18 percent in 2005 to an anticipated 25 percent in 2030. By contrast, the U.S.'s share (not energy use) is projected to dip down to 17 percent in 2030. How will the world meet its inhabitants' rising demands without further endangering the planet?

Here in America, our electric energy is mainly supplied by coal, which accounted for 49 percent of all electricity generation in 2007. Natural gas ranked second at 20 percent, with nuclear following closely behind at 19.4 percent. Hydroelectric power from dams accounts for 7 percent of all electricity generation, while other renewable energies like solar and wind powered 2.4 percent of our needs. Petroleum provides just a small sliver of our electric supply (1.6 percent).

There is much debate today over how to expand the country's energy scope. Should it be obtained through more nuclear power plants? Do we invest in additional coal mines? Or, does a focus on sustainable energy sources such as solar and wind power—that don't continue to bellow CO_2 emissions and also rely on and exhaust our fossil fuel stores—make the most sense?

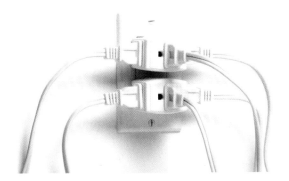

Americans consume almost one-quarter of the world's energy supply. ©istockphoto.com/Eric Hood

The Pros and Cons of Conventional Energy Sources

DOES ELECTRICITY AFFECT the environment? The answer is a resounding "yes"—all sources do have some level of impact, although some are much more significant than others. The emissions produced from generating electricity account for the largest chunk of U.S. greenhouse gases (almost 40 percent), even more than transportation, which contributes about one-third of the carbon dioxide produced by the U.S.

In addition, the reality is that many of these resources are limited; fossil fuels are considered non-renewable resources because they took millions of years to form and cannot be replenished in a human timeframe.

Coal-fired power plants are the largest producer of greenhouse gases in the U.S.
©istockphoto.com/pixelmaniak

The following list covers the ups and downs of the fuels that keep our home fires burning. Armed with information, you can weigh the energy debate for yourself.

▶ **Coal: This fossil fuel was created by ancient plant materials, which contained carbon formed from photosynthesis, that decomposed and were subsequently formed by pressure and geologic heat. To be transformed into energy, it must be mined, transported, and burned in power plants to produce steam that generates electricity. Pros: The U.S. has enormous coal reserves— more than any other country—that stand at 275 billion tons, an amount capable of meeting domestic demand for more than 250 years at current consumption rates. In addition, it is one of the least expensive energy sources for consumers. Cons: Coal-fired power plants are the biggest producers of climate-affecting greenhouse gases in the U.S. A wicked brew is released into the air when coal is burned, including carbon dioxide, sulfur dioxide, nitrogen oxides, and mercury compounds. Coal mining can also be devastating to the environment. Strip mining degrades natural ecosystems and displaces wildlife; mountaintop removal mining actually employs explosives to remove up to 1,000 vertical feet of a mountaintop to gain access to coal seams below.**

▶ **Natural Gas:** Another fossil fuel, natural gas was formed from the effects of pressure and heat to the earth's layers of buried plants and animals. The primary component of natural gas is methane. It is extracted, treated, and transported to power plants, where it lands in combustion boilers to create electricity. **Pros:** The world's supplies of natural gas are also plentiful and much is believed to be still undiscovered. The Energy Information Administration estimates the world's natural gas reserves to be around 5,210 trillion cubic feet, of which 3 percent lies in the U.S. In 2005, the world used just over 100 trillion cubic feet. In addition, natural gas burns about 50 percent cleaner than coal, meaning it produces fewer greenhouse gases. **Cons:** The burning of natural gas still produces nitrogen oxides and carbon dioxide, which are emitted into the earth's atmosphere. Certain drilling methods have also caused some environmental concerns over affects on water supply quality.

Around the world, no new nuclear plants have been built since 1996. ©istockphoto.com/Hans F. Meier

▶ **Nuclear:** Nuclear energy is created when uranium atoms are split in a process called fission, which produces steam that powers turbines to create energy. Uranium is a non-renewable resource that is extracted from open-pit and underground mines. **Pros:** Nuclear power plants do not emit the greenhouse gas carbon dioxide or even sulfur dioxide and nitrogen oxides. In fact, some sources say that nuclear-generated electricity curtails the emissions of about 700 million metric tons of carbon dioxide per year in the U.S. **Cons:** While the reactors produce few greenhouse gases, the nuclear fuel cycle (including mining and transport) does emit these dangerous gases. Additionally, the U.S.'s nuclear plants produce about 2,000 metric tons of radioactive waste each year that must be safely stored—it remains armed and dangerous for thousands of years. The radioactive nature of this power source also poses a danger to the public with the possibility of malfunctions and meltdowns.

Eco Fact

Because burning coal provides nearly all of Wyoming's electrical power, on a per-person basis, this Western state produces more carbon dioxide than any other state—or any other country.

▶ **Oil:** This fossil fuel is used primarily for fueling our modes of transport and home heaters, but a small percentage is utilized as fuel to generate electricity. Found in underground reservoirs, it is also a product of organic materials that have decomposed and been subjected to heat and pressure over millions of years. It is obtained by drilling crude oil from deep wells; it is then refined and shipped to a power plant for use in a combustion turbine. **Pros:** Until recently, oil has appeared to be an inexpensive, easily obtained resource. **Cons:** Many experts believe this non-renewable resource has reached peak production and the world's stores are running out. A future of waning supplies is projected to equate to skyrocketing prices, limited availability, and world unrest. In addition, burning oil at power plants produces a massive blend of greenhouse gases, including carbon dioxide, methane, sulfur dioxide, and nitrogen oxides.

Green Idea

Want to see how your state stacks up against the other 49 when it comes to carbon emissions caused by power generation? Check out http://www.epa.gov/cleanenergy/energy-and-you/chart-text.html.

Eco Fact

A test plant in Spremberg, Germany, is aspiring to make "clean coal" power by burning brown coal with pure oxygen, rather than air, which produces nearly pure carbon dioxide emissions. These are then condensed, liquefied, and pumped into a long-term storage space (in the future, it is hoped oil gas fields or salt aquifers miles below the earth's surface will serve this purpose). If proven to work in trials, the much-talked-about clean coal could be rolled out to turn coal into a much cleaner fuel. Environmental activists have voiced concerns that this technology, which has not been adequately studied, will divert efforts away from the truly clean, renewable energy resources.

Did You Know?

Greenhouse gases are key ingredients in the earth's atmosphere; they absorb and emit radiation, which bounces off the earth's surface, clouds, and the atmosphere itself. Greenhouse gases are essential to maintaining the temperature of the earth—without them, the planet would be so cold as to be uninhabitable. It is, however, a finely tuned balance. An excess of greenhouse gases turns up the heat and could cause the earth to be too hot for life to survive, as it is on Venus, where high levels of carbon dioxide create a surface temperature of almost 900 degrees Fahrenheit.

The Thing About Clean Power

AS YOU CAN SEE, energy produced from fossil fuels has a host of issues, which is exactly why power produced from renewable resources that are free of greenhouse gas emissions is called "clean" power. Energy sources like solar power from the sun and wind power are in constant supply and are, thus, sustainable sources that are not likely to run out.

While hydroelectric energy has been in play for over a century, wind and solar are newer energy sources that are quickly catching on because of their clean, green appeal. Here is a look at the pros and cons of the major renewable energy sources today:

▶ **Solar Power:** What energy source could be more abundant than the sun? Solar power converts the power of the sun's light into energy via photovoltaic systems (where wafers made of silicon react to the sun to create electricity) and solar-thermal technologies, which use mirrors to heat a liquid that produces steam used to generate electricity. **Pros:** Sunlight is a renewable resource and no fuels are combusted during energy production with solar power, so no emissions are created. The potential for this resource is immense; according to *Scientific American*, the energy in the sunlight that strikes the earth for 40 minutes is equal to the entire human race's energy needs for one year. Additionally, more efficient and affordable solar cells are currently in development; the cost of solar is expected to decline as demand increases. **Cons:** Solar arrays are growing as an energy source in the U.S., but there is a long way to go before they can supply enough to meet our energy demands.

While solar is a more expensive energy source today, a new study reveals that cost parity with other sources will be achieved by 2025. ©istockphoto.com/Kativ

▶ **Wind Power:** The creation of wind is a simple process; it is formed when the various seasons and cloud cover cause the sun to heat the Earth unevenly. Wind turbines scoop up wind with two or three long blades; the movement of the turbine is converted, through a generator, into electricity. **Pros:** Wind is renewable and emissions-free. Again, no fossil fuels are burned so no greenhouse gases are created. **Cons:** Wind power is also in its infancy and is in limited supply in the U.S. There is also some environmental concern that birds and bats are being killed when they run into the turbine's blades.

In 2006, wind farms in the U.S. generated enough electricity to supply more than 2.4 million households with power. ©istockphoto.com/Sabrina dei nobili

▶ **Hydroelectricity:** This renewable energy resource utilizes the earth's continuous water cycle. The kinetic energy created by the movement of water flowing downstream can be converted into electricity via a hydroelectric power plant. Here, water (which is typically held at a dam) is forced through a turbine connected to a generator. In the Pacific Northwest, hydropower supplies two-thirds of the area's electricity needs. **Pros:** Hydropower has no air quality impacts, namely harmful greenhouse gas emissions. It is also tied to water, a renewable resource that is unlike coal or gas, which are in limited reserve. **Cons:** Hydropower dams can significantly impact natural river systems, including the fish and wildlife populations there.

The hydroelectric plant at Hoover Dam is one of the world's largest producers of electric power.

Buying Clean Power Locally

NOW THAT YOU KNOW all the good reasons why clean power simply makes sense for the planet, you can continue to travel along your green journey by investing in it yourself. No need to go out and tack some solar panels to your roof or raise a wind turbine in the back yard just yet. Greening your energy can be as simple as calling your local electric company.

Many utility companies today sell power supplied by renewable resources for a small monthly premium. For example, in Colorado, La Plata Electric Association, Inc. delivers a green energy choice for customers who want to buy some or all of their electricity from "clean" sources. This is offered in 100 kilowatt-hour (kWh) blocks that each cost an additional 80 cents a month.

Green Idea

Today, another local energy option exists. Because electricity markets are now fully or partly open to competition in more than a dozen states, Green Power marketers have emerged to sell Green Power in the competitive marketplace. These marketers exist in the District of Columbia, California, Illinois, Maryland, New Jersey, New York, Pennsylvania, Texas, Virginia, and a number of New England states. For more information, see: http://apps3.eere.energy.gov/greenpower/markets/marketing.shtml?page=1.

Cost Meter (per month): $

Electricity created from wind power is renewable and emissions-free. ©istockphoto.com/DSGpro

The typical U.S. household consumes about 11,000 kWh per year, according to the U.S. Department of Energy. At this rate, it would cost about $9 a month to convert to green energy with La Plata Electric. According to the U.S. Department of Energy, Green Power programs across the country range in cost from less than one cent per kWh to five cents per kWh. An impressive amount of local utilities offer its customers this option. Their clean power commitments include everything from solar photovoltaic and wind power to landfill gas, geothermal, and hydropower. The blocks you purchase will be delivered to the general utility grid and help promote the demand and development of renewable energy sources.

For a complete listing of green utility programs by state, check out the U.S. Department of Energy's informational website at: http://apps3.eere.energy.gov/greenpower/markets/pricing.shtml?page=1.

Switching to CFLs

A SIMPLE AND ILLUMINATING green step you can take to make your home's energy more earth-friendly is to swap out your traditional incandescent light bulbs with newer, energy-efficient compact fluorescent lamps (CFLs). These use 75 percent less energy, a substantial electricity savings that will equate to lower electricity bills and a clearer conscience as you do your part to help reduce greenhouse gas emissions. In fact, according to the EPA's ENERGY STAR program, if every homeowner in the U.S. replaced just one traditional light bulb with an ENERGY STAR qualified bulb like a CFL, we would prevent greenhouse emissions equivalent to taking over 800,000 cars off the road.

Lighting costs account for about 20 percent of the average U.S. household's energy bill, so buying and installing long-lasting, energy-efficient CFLs in your home could deliver some serious savings. On average, compact fluorescent bulbs last about 10 to 15 times longer than traditional bulbs. They do cost about three to four times more than incandescent bulbs (at about $6 to $7 each). ENERGY STAR estimates that homeowners will save about $30 or more in electricity costs over each bulb's lifetime, meaning they will more than pay for themselves. If replacing all your light bulbs at once is too costly or daunting, simply replace the incandescent bulbs in your most-used lights with CFLs. This will make a big difference and you can replace the rest over time as the older, traditional bulbs burn out.

Cost Meter: **$ $**

(over time, this change will save you money)

Joining the CFL revolution will help green your energy.
©istockphoto.com/Janine Lamontagne

CFLs fit right into regular light sockets and they can be found at most home improvement retailers and even some supermarkets in your area. This earth-friendly light bulb comes in a variety of colors and watt ratings. All ENERGY STAR qualified CFLs must pass extensive testing to ensure they produce the highest-quality light. If you prefer the light similar to that given off by incandescent bulbs, choose ENERGY STAR qualified CFLs labeled "warm white" or "soft white."

Of note is that, by 2012, all light bulbs will be required to use 30 percent less energy than today's incandescent bulbs. This ruling is courtesy of the Energy Independence and Security Act of 2007 (i.e., the "Energy Bill"), signed by President Bush. By 2020, all bulbs will be required to be at least 70 percent more efficient (equal to today's CFLs). Light-emitting diodes (LEDs) are another, greener lighting option and some last as long as 60,000 hours but these bulbs are costly and current options do not emit the type of light most homeowners are looking for. They are best suited to reading lamps or under-cabinet lighting.

If you're making the move to CFLs, you can also make your green voice heard by signing the ENERGY STAR program's *Change a Light, Change the World* pledge to change at least one light at home to an ENERGY STAR qualified light. So far, nearly two million Americans have signed the pledge, helping to reduce greenhouse gas emissions by over 3.5 billion pounds. Sign up at www.energystar.gov.

In addition, while incandescent bulbs can be tossed in the trash, CFLs must be recycled because they contain a small amount of mercury. The EPA recommends that consumers handle the bulbs carefully (trying not to break them) and recycle them at appropriate locations. These can be located by checking out epa.gov/bulbrecycling. Locally, retailers like Home Depot, Ace Hardware, and IKEA all offer CFL recycling programs.

Green Idea

If your CFL burns out before two years, you are entitled to a refund. All manufacturers producing ENERGY STAR qualified CFLs are required to offer at least a two-year limited warranty to those installing them in the home. If your CFL takes a hike, take a look at the base, find the manufacturer's name, and visit their website to locate the customer service contact information to inquire about a refund or replacement. Be sure to hang onto your receipts for all CFL purchases.

The One-Degree Difference

ONE OF THE SIMPLEST GREEN steps you can take is also one that will save you money. In the end, it also reduces energy consumption, greenhouse gas emissions, and the burden on the planet. According to the EIA, households that lower their thermostats by just one degree Fahrenheit during the winter could save a bundle in heating costs. With heating bills rising across the country, energy consumers can take matters into their own hands by placing them on the thermostat and notching it down just a bit.

By turning the thermostat down one degree from the temperature you normally set it at, some estimates suggest you could save 3 percent of your total energy use. If your winter heating bills ring in at an average of $150 a month, you could stand to save $30 over the course of the season. In ten years, you've saved more than $300. If you can lower your temp by two or three degrees, the savings really start to add up. In the end, the cost savings you may realize will also depend on the main type and typical amount of heating fuel your home uses.

Cost Meter: $0
(this change will save you money)

With a one-degree drop on the thermostat, those homes that are heated by natural gas would consume 5 percent less fuel and those running on electricity would use 6 percent less. If your house uses more costly fuel oil, the savings would ring in at 4 percent. Those utilizing kerosene or LPG would save 5 percent. On the flip side, those with air conditioning can inch their thermostat up a degree in the summertime to realize energy savings year round.

Will you feel the difference of one degree in temperature? Perhaps not, but the planet will.
©istockphoto.com/Ben Beltman

Green Ideas

If you've got the inclination, taking a few other simple energy-saving measures could greatly reduce your energy bills and your share of greenhouse gas emissions:

* **Step it back at night:** Toss on an extra blanket and set your thermostat back as much as five degrees every night when you go to sleep. You can also turn down the heat when you leave home for a vacation or work trip.

* **Throw a party:** And turn off the heat. Each guest generates heat equivalent to that of a 175-watt heater; a large group will undoubtedly heat things up.

* **Install an ENERGY STAR qualified programmable thermostat:** The four pre-programmed temperature settings allow you to fine-tune your energy needs and save about $100 each year, according to the EPA.

* **Replace or clean furnace filters monthly:** This, plus regular lubrication and tune-ups can save another 5 percent on your heating bill.

States and Energy

* According to the EIA, the top five energy-consuming states are, in order, Texas, California, New York, Florida, and Pennsylvania.

* The states that expend the least energy? The District of Columbia, Vermont, South Dakota, Delaware, and Rhode Island.

* Hawaii has the highest energy prices; it is closely followed by the District of Columbia. The lowest prices are found in North Dakota.

* Alaska and Wyoming have the highest energy expenditures per capita; Utah has the lowest.

Powering Down

DID YOUR PARENTS ALWAYS yell at you to turn the lights off around the house when they weren't in use? Today, their cost-consciousness could also equate to a proactive eco-conscious nature. Since electricity typically burns up fossil fuels for energy, you can help reduce carbon emissions simply by turning off lights and powering down appliances when you're not actively using them.

On their own, household electronics account for almost 5 percent of the average home's energy bill. But, most of these items still continue to draw a small amount of energy even when they are switched off. Would you believe that 75 percent of the electricity used to power home electronics is linked to items that are actually turned off?

Cost Meter: $0
(this change will save you money)

According to the U.S. Department of Energy, this energy flow can be avoided by unplugging these and other appliances directly—or corralling them together in one power strip and using its switch to turn everything off when not in use.

Just say "no" to power when it's not needed. A power strip makes it easy to turn off many appliances all at once. ©istockphoto.com/tioloco

GREEN ON THE CHEAP

These tips, also discussed in Chapter 2, "Ten Simple Steps," will help you unplug the most effective items in the home when they are not being used—and save some money doing it:

- **Unplug seldom-used appliances:** Got a fridge in the garage that's cooling just a few sodas? Transfer your drinks to the main fridge and unplug its garage counterpart. You could even save up to $10 a month on your utility bill.

- **Unplug chargers when you're done charging:** No doubt, you have an array of plastic power chargers to keep your cell phones, PDAs, and digital cameras up and running. If they're plugged in they're using power. Keep them unplugged until you need them.

- **Turn off the tube:** Even at rest (i.e., turned off), your TVs, DVD players, VCRs, and stereos are sucking energy. All together, their "standby" consumption can be equal to that of a 100-watt light bulb running continuously. One quick way to turn them all off when you're leaving the house is to connect them to a single power strip.

- **Set computers to sleep:** Enabling the "sleep mode" feature for periods of inactivity on your computer can make a huge difference in its energy consumption. In Windows, the power management settings are found on your computer's Control Panel. Mac users can look for energy-saving settings under "System Preferences" in the Apple menu.

—Information courtesy NRDC

Offsetting Your Energy Use

I F YOU ARE UNABLE to purchase Green Power through your local utility company—or you'd simply like to invest in even more—you can purchase Renewable Energy Certificates (RECs). Also known as Green Tags, Tradable Renewable Certificates (TRCs), or Renewable Energy Credits, these certificates are tradable environmental commodities that each represent one megawatt-hour (MWh) of electricity produced by a renewable energy resource such as wind turbines, hydropower plants, and solar arrays.

Wind power is one clean, renewable energy source that can be purchased through Renewable Energy Certificates. ©istockphoto.com/Alexander Hafemann

Cost Meter: **$ $ $** to **$ $ $ $**

If you purchase a REC, you only receive a certificate. The renewable energy that is related to each REC is actually produced and fed back into the grid; it does not go directly to any one home or business. Each REC boasts a unique number, given by a certifying agency, which ensures each MWh is only counted and sold once. If you purchase a REC, however, it is an item you can resell; whoever is in possession of the REC is the "owner" of that particular renewable energy.

The bottom line is that the purchase of RECs helps to finance renewable resource energy production. Each MWh of clean energy produced reduces the need for the production of the same amount of pollution—and emissions-causing conventional power. The more support renewable energy forms receive, the more they can grow and extend their carbon-neutral reach.

How can you be sure your RECs are coming from a reliable, verified source? An excellent place to start when buying these types of credits is with the Green-e certification program, which is operated by the Center for Resource Solutions. Green-e (www.green-e.org) is a leading independent consumer protection program that oversees the sale of renewable energy (plus greenhouse gas emission reductions) in the retail market. This program's website has a search feature that enables you to look for renewable energy certificate options by location and renewable resource type.

You can also go directly to the source and check out the REC options from providers such as www.3degreesinc.com and www.nativeenergy.com. While costs vary, the average price for enough RECs to balance the carbon footprint of a small home for a year is about $96.

Things to consider when buying RECs include:

▶ **The type of renewable resource it represents.**

▶ **The percent of various renewables.**

▶ **The price.**

▶ **The location, if this is important to you for proximity to your home or state.**

Green Idea

You can also shop green and spend your money at stores that support clean energy technologies. Many retailers are saving on energy costs and boosting their environmental profiles by adding solar panels to their roofs. Wal-Mart has installed solar panels in 17 of its stores and distribution centers with plans for more in the near future. Macy's is in the process of installing solar panels in 40 stores and Safeway is doing it in 23. Kohl's is also going solar in a whopping 85 stores.

Green Review: Things to Do During Week Two

1. Buy clean power locally through your area's utility company.

2. Install energy-saving CFLs in all of your home's light fixtures or simply the most-used.

3. Set your thermostat just one degree lower in the winter to conserve energy resources, reduce emissions, and save on your energy bill.

4. Completely power down and unplug your appliances and chargers when not in use.

5. If you are inspired by clean energy or don't have the option available via your local utility, offset your energy use and support renewable sources by purchasing Renewable Energy Certificates.

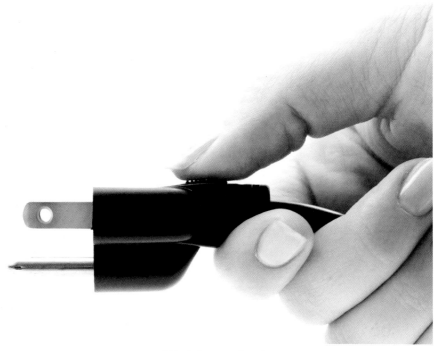

©istockphoto.com/ranplett

TrueGreen: Go with ENERGY STAR

IF YOU WANT TO TAKE bigger steps to green your energy use you can, both today and in the future, replace your old or broken electronics with earth-friendly, energy-efficient models that are ENERGY STAR qualified. ENERGY STAR, which is sponsored jointly by the U.S. Environmental Protection Agency and the U.S. Department of Energy, was set up in 1992 as a voluntary labeling program to help Americans save money and reduce greenhouse gas emissions through energy-efficient products and lifestyle choices. The first labeled products were computers and monitors.

Buying products that feature the ENERGY STAR logo ensures you are making the best choice for the planet.
©ENERGY STAR

Today, ENERGY STAR qualifies a vast array of consumer products, from washing machines and PDAs to new homes, but only those that meet strict energy efficiency guidelines set by the EPA and U.S. Department of Energy. These government organizations say that Americans using ENERGY STAR qualified products in 2007 alone saved an impressive $16 billion on energy bills while also avoiding greenhouse gas emissions equal to those from 27 million cars (40 million metric tons).

If you are looking for a new household product, —or any energy-requiring item, for that matter— look for the ENERGY STAR seal to help you make the right choice for the planet. About 2,000 manufacturers use the ENERGY STAR label to differentiate more than 40,000 individual product models. Today, there is much choice within the program and consumers do not have to sacrifice quality, functionality, or style to save energy.

In 2007, Americans purchased more than 500 million ENERGY STAR qualified products in categories ranging from appliances and consumer electronics to heating and cooling systems, lighting, and office equipment. Additionally, over 120,000 new homes were constructed in 2007 that met ENERGY STAR guidelines. The program states that those consumers looking to ENERGY STAR for the most efficient products and energy-saving practices can save up to 30 percent per year on their utility bills.

Tax credits may also be on the horizon for you if you are making significant home improvements that include new ENERGY STAR qualified windows, doors, metal roofs, central air conditioning, furnaces, or boilers. On October 3rd, 2008, President Bush signed the Emergency Economic Stabilization Act of 2008 into law, which included an extension for energy-efficient home improvements made January 1st through December 31st, 2009. For more information, see http://www.energystar.gov/index.cfm?c=products.pr_tax_credits.

Green on the Cheap

Buying ENERGY STAR can save you:

- $550 in operating costs for a qualified clothes washer over its lifetime.

- More than $30 a year in utility costs for a qualified dishwasher.

- About 30% utility savings for a qualified television versus a standard model.

- Approximately $250 in operating costs over the life of a qualified dehumidifier.

Want to know your home's energy score?

Check out the following websites for easy, do-it-yourself energy audits:

- **EPA Home Energy Yardstick:** http://www.energystar.gov/index.cfm?fuseaction=home_energy_yardstick.showStep2

- **ENERGY STAR Home Advisor:** http://www.energystar.gov/index.cfm?fuseaction=home_energy_advisor.showGetInput

- **The U.S. Department of Energy's Home Energy Saver audit:** (http://www.hes.lbl.gov)

- **Other easy home audit information and energy-saving tips are available from the U.S. Department of Energy at** http://apps1.eere.energy.gov/consumer/your_home/energy_audits/index.cfm/mytopic=11170

SuperGreen: Perform an Energy Audit

IF YOU'VE GOT the time and you aspire to be supremely green, a home energy audit can help you pinpoint your household systems' strengths and weaknesses. Since our electricity use contributes greatly to greenhouse gas emissions, reducing the amount your home consumes by increasing its efficiency will do a whole lot of good for the planet.

It's simple to perform a do-it-yourself audit that is free and easy. Or, you can choose to invest in an audit performed by a qualified professional. Either way, you'll save money in the long run by lowering your utility bills.

Both the EPA and the U.S. Department of Energy offer excellent do-it-yourself audit information through their websites. The EPA delivers a quick Home Energy Yardstick that measures your home's energy use—and how it stacks up against that of other U.S. homeowners. You'll need your last 12 months of utility bills and about five minutes.

The Department of Energy offers a more in-depth Home Energy Saver audit that was developed by researchers at Berkeley Lab's Environmental Energy Technologies Division. It helps users identify the best ways to save energy in their homes and also find the resources to make the necessary changes. It also calculates how much you can reduce your emissions by putting energy-efficient changes into play. About 750,000 people visit this site each year.

On the other side, when you receive a professional energy audit, you will be provided with very specific recommendations for improving your own home's energy efficiency. An energy auditor will perform a thorough assessment of your home, typically using special equipment such as blower doors, which measure the extent of leaks, and infrared cameras, which uncover leaks and areas with spotty insulation. Contact your utility company; many offer free or discounted energy audits.

You can also hire an auditor, such as a certified Home Energy Rater, to assess the situation and help you make positive changes. Look in your yellow pages under "Energy" for a qualified professional; be sure to confirm their total cost and ask for references. Fees range from about $200 to $300, but you will recoup this money within a year if you are making the recommended energy efficiency changes.

Are solar panels in your future? For now, a home energy audit will help make your home cleaner and greener. ©istockphoto.com/jim pruitt

An organic apple a day just might keep the doctor away. © istockphoto.com/Skip ODonnell

Week Three: Green Your Appetite

5

WHO DOESN'T LOVE A CRISP APPLE, a handful of fresh blueberries, a crunchy ear of corn, or even a buttery baked potato? While these foods sound like nutritious, healthy choices, they actually might not be if they were grown with conventional farming methods.

A harmful secret lurks in the aisles of your grocery store. It affects the vast majority of the fresh and processed foods sold there. And, it infiltrates our bodies, soaks into our soils, and seeps into our groundwater. This invisible enigma has a powerful name—pesticides.

Even the Environmental Protection Agency (EPA) acknowledges that there are serious human health and environmental risks associated with traditional chemical pesticides used in farming today. But, fear not, there are some simple, low-cost solutions to ensuring a healthy future for you, your family, and the planet.

This chapter provides information about pesticides and looks at simple alternatives, such as pesticide-free, organic foods, to help maintain the health of the planet and its inhabitants. It also delves into the earth-friendly reasons for buying local, looks at the benefits of filtering your drinking water, and even delivers suggestions for the healthiest and most sustainable fish, meat, and milk to buy on your next grocery trip. All with an eye to keeping the costs of greening your appetite low. Hungry (or thirsty) yet? This week your green journey is a culinary one.

The Pesticide Proliferation

THE U.S. GEOLOGICAL Survey estimates that approximately one billion pounds of pesticides are used in the United States each year. In addition, nearly 10,000 different pesticides are permitted for use in the U.S. The pesticides used on food crops include insecticides to control insects, rodenticides to control rodents, herbicides to control weeds, fungicides to control mold and fungus, and antimicrobials to control bacteria. Altogether, these create a complex soup of chemicals that are sprayed right onto our food as it grows. Many argue that pesticides are a necessary risk that helps grow an adequate, economical supply of food to enable the fast-growing population of the world to be fed. But, today an increasing number of health-savvy consumers are choosing to bypass the pesticides in their foods and opt for organic produce and meats instead.

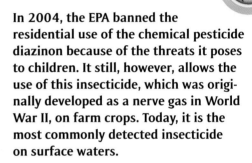

Eco Fact

In 2004, the EPA banned the residential use of the chemical pesticide diazinon because of the threats it poses to children. It still, however, allows the use of this insecticide, which was originally developed as a nerve gas in World War II, on farm crops. Today, it is the most commonly detected insecticide on surface waters.

Even though U.S. cropland acreage has decreased over the years, U.S. pesticide use saw a marked increase, from 900 million pounds in 1992 to 940 million pounds in 2000, according to a report by the U.S. General Accounting Office. The worst fertilizing offenders to our health—including organophosphates, carbamates, and probable carcinogens—accounted for over 40 percent of the pesticides used in U.S. agriculture.

A crop duster covers a conventional farm's crops with pesticides. ©istockphoto.com/Greg Gardner

While the EPA does set limits for just how much pesticide residue can remain on our foods, some amount is still ingested when you eat non-organic produce. In addition, the USDA recently pulled the plug on an 18-year-old program that tests the levels of pesticides in fruits, vegetables, and field crops, saying that its $8 million yearly cost was too expensive. The information from this government program, the Agricultural Chemical Usage Program, was used by the EPA to set safe levels of pesticides in food.

Who, if not our own government, will monitor the presence of the pesticides present in our own food? The EPA says it will look to expensive, privately collected data for answers but the Union of Concerned Scientists have called these data sets "unreliable."

Are there really safe levels of pesticides that can enter our bodies? A Centers for Disease Control and Prevention report released in 2001 stated that "measurable amounts" of organophosphate pesticide metabolites were found in all the people who were part of the study. The report also noted that, at the time, organophosphate pesticides accounted for approximately half of all the insecticides used in the U.S.

Because of their higher metabolisms and lower body weights, children and infants can be more at risk to the effects of pesticides in our food supply. A 1998 report from the Environmental Working Group stated that every day, more than one million children aged five and under (one out of 20), ingest combinations of 13 different neurotoxic insecticides, including an unsafe dose of organophosphate insecticide, through the food they eat. Commercial baby food was the culprit for infants aged six to twelve months; the report said it exposes about 77,000 infants to pesticides each day.

A worker in a protective suit sprays fertilizer on strawberry crops. ©istockphoto.com/David T Gomez

Even the growing fetuses of pregnant women can be affected by pesticides. A study released in 2005 revealed that the umbilical-cord blood of 10 children, which was collected by the Red Cross and tested for pollutants, showed that 21 pesticides had crossed the placenta, in addition to over 250 other industrial chemicals and pollutants.

It's clear that you are what you eat. But, what are the actual effects of putting pesticides into your body? Short-term problems can include headaches, nausea, and fatigue. According to the Environmental Working Group, well-designed animal studies have shown that pesticide exposure also causes a laundry list of more serious health effects, ranging from cancer and nervous system damage to reproductive effects.

The EPA's website states, "Pesticides can cause harm to humans, animals, or the environment because they are designed to kill or otherwise adversely affect living organisms." Now, that's food for thought.

Eco Fact

A yearlong, peer-reviewed study released in 2008 found that urine and saliva samples taken from children eating a variety of conventional foods contained organophosphates, the genre of pesticides related to the nerve gas agents created in World War II. The main pesticides found were malathion and chlorpyrifos. The latter is one of the most widely used organophosphate insecticides in the U.S. Chlorpyrifos' maker, Dow Chemical Co., pulled the pesticide voluntarily from the residential market after studies showed that children were often exposed to enormously high doses. It has potentially serious health effects—animal research shows that chlorpyrifos affects brain development and behavior.

On its website, the EPA gives a nod to the "special susceptibility and sensitivity of children to developmental and neurological effects from exposure to chlorpyrifos." Still, this harmful chemical makes its way into our food system. The upside of the study is that when the same test group of children (ages 3 to 11) ate a diet of organic fruits, vegetables, and juices, all signs of pesticides disappeared within 8 to 36 hours. When their normal conventional diets were reintroduced, the pesticide levels were again present in saliva and urine samples. The researchers, who found pesticide levels to be higher in the winter when more produce is imported, have voiced concerns that imports are not being monitored adequately for safe pesticide levels.

Are the foods your kids are eating safe for consumption?
©istockphoto.com/ Nicole S. Young

Pesticides and the Environment

FOOD ISN'T THE only vehicle for pesticides to enter our bodies. A 2006 USGS report on pesticide use detected pesticides in more than 90 percent of all streams sampled. The study also looked into wells, showing that more than half of shallow wells and a full third of deeper wells revealed the presence of at least one pesticide. This same study found almost all fish samples taken to contain pesticides as well, meaning that our fertilizing habits are affecting wildlife as well.

In Oregon, one of the first states to make a concerted effort to study its pesticide use and effects, water samples taken by the Oregon Department of Environmental Quality and the U.S. Geological Survey showed that seven pesticides appeared routinely, including chlorpyrifos and diazinon.

Catching Their Drift: In 2007, air monitoring near South Woods Elementary School in Hastings, Florida, detected four agricultural chemicals in the air, often at levels that pose significant health risks to children. The school is located in an agricultural area adjacent to fields of Chinese cabbage. The pesticide of greatest concern, called endosulfan, was found in 87 percent of the air samples, many of which exceeded acceptable levels. The test revealed the air to be contaminated with the pesticides endosulfan, diazinon, trifluralin, and chlorothalonil—two of which are neurotoxins and three that are (or will soon be) banned in Europe.

In addition to affecting the earth's water supply, pesticides stake their claim in our soils. A study published in 2000 showed that some illegal pesticides, many of which can lead to digestive and nervous system disorders, continue to show up in the food supply for decades after they were banned. As part of the study, researchers planted a garden in ground heavily treated with chlordane 38 years earlier. They found chlordane residues in all 12 of the vegetables planted, including potatoes, lettuce, and carrots.

Many of the same pesticides that affect our water and land also waft into the air supply. Geoscientists at Texas A&M University found that air pollutants can even be transported over long distances through wind, rain, and evaporation. They actually found high levels of pesticides present in beluga whales from the Arctic, where the chemicals have never been used.

A 1999 study found that more than 90 percent of water and fish samples from streams contained pesticides. ©istockphoto.com/Nicolas McComber

Going Organic

OW FOR THE GOOD NEWS. There is an option to conventional foods grown with harmful pesticides. Organically grown food is grown and processed using no synthetic fertilizers or pesticides. Which is exactly why an increasing number of consumers are purchasing certified organic foods today. You can also step away from pesticides, ditch the insecticides, and feel more confident about the health of your family by choosing to add organic foods into your diet.

Some studies have even found organic foods to be more nutritious, offering more of some nutrients like vitamin C, iron, magnesium, and phosphorus. A report from University of Florida researchers and The Organic Center determined that organic foods contain, on average, 25 percent higher concentrations of 11 nutrients than their conventional counterparts.

Biting into organic foods will greatly reduce your exposure to pesticides. ©istockphoto.com/Evelin Elmest

Cost Meter: **$** to **$$**

When Congress passed the Organic Foods Production Act of 1990, there was just under one million acres of certified organic farmland in the U.S. That's a space just slightly larger than the state of Rhode Island. The country's organic acreage had doubled by the time the USDA implemented national organic standards in 2002 and it doubled again by the time 2005 rolled around. In fact, in 2005, for the first time ever, all 50 states boasted some certified organic farming, including organic livestock programs, which have also grown rapidly over the last two decades.

In 2006, organic food sales rang in $17 billion in sales, representing about 3 percent of all retail sales of food and beverages. This number has grown steadily and is up from 1.9 percent in 2003.

The USDA organic logo was developed to give consumers confidence that organic products have consistent, uniform standards. ©USDA

When you see the official USDA Organic label or a product that is "Certified Organic" you can rest assured that what you are buying truly is organic because all producers and handlers must be certified by a USDA-accredited certifying agent to sell, label, or represent their products with one of the following monikers: "100 percent organic," "organic," or "made with organic specified ingredients or food group(s)." Organic livestock products are classified as such because the animal was fed organic feed and did not receive antibiotics.

Organic agriculture is typically more cost-intensive than conventional agriculture, so farmers count on garnering higher prices for their food to cover their costs. There is definitely a price difference with organic food—premiums in 2004 for produce such as apples, grapes, strawberries, and tomatoes were about $0.35/lb. more than their conventional counterparts. Many believe that as organic farming becomes more prolific, these prices will begin to drop.

To keep this green step cost-efficient, simply add more organic products into your diet; not everything must be organic. In fact, the next few pages provide information on the best bets for your money when buying organic.

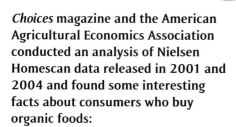

Eco Facts

Choices magazine and the American Agricultural Economics Association conducted an analysis of Nielsen Homescan data released in 2001 and 2004 and found some interesting facts about consumers who buy organic foods:

- Of all regions in the U.S., households in the Western region spent the most per capita on organic produce.

- Asian and African-American consumers choose organic over conventional produce more than White or Hispanic consumers.

- No consistent positive associations were found between household income and expenditures on organic produce.

Did You Know?

Since the rise of organic foods and agribusiness' embrace of all things organic, from lettuce to Oreos, some environmentalists have been crying, "Wolf." As consumer demand heightens for organics, there is concern that it could launch a very unsustainable, fossil-fuel-heavy business platform if organic kiwis are shipped from New Zealand and organic olives make their way from Italy. This has launched a grand scale debate about the merits of organic foods versus local foods. Buying local, organic food is a win-win for every person looking to green their lifestyle. If given the choice, many say that local foods are better for the planet, especially since many local farmers use sustainable, pesticide-free practices anyway. In the end, the decision where to put your money is up to you.

The Most Bang for Your Organic Buck

WHILE IT MAY BE APPEALING, switching your diet over to all organic foods could be a significant cost investment. If you're inspired to take the plunge, more power to you. Those who would like to keep their grocery bills from increasing by up to 50 percent can follow some advice from the Environmental Working Group (EWG), which has pinpointed the most important fruits and vegetables to buy organic.

In fact, the EWG performed a simulation with thousands of consumers eating both high- and low-pesticide diets. The results? The EWG determined that people could lower their own pesticide exposure by nearly 90 percent by simply swapping out the top twelve most-contaminated fruits and vegetables for organic varieties.

When you're in the mood for juicy, red strawberries, head straight for the organic section.
©istockphoto.com/Dean Turner

Check out the lists on the next page from the EWG's "Shopper's Guide to Pesticides in Produce" to help plan your next pesticide-reducing grocery run. This list is based on the analysis of nearly 51,000 tests conducted on food from 2001 to 2005 to determine its pesticide levels.

Interestingly, a variety of fruits were at the top of the EWG's high-in-pesticides list. Nectarines were the worst offenders, followed by peaches and apples. According to the EWG, samples of peaches and apples revealed up to nine pesticides and samples of strawberries showed traces of eight different pesticides.

On the veggie side, sweet bell peppers boasted an incredible 11 pesticides on a single sample, while celery and lettuce came in tied for second with nine pesticides detected. For a printable list of this invaluable guide, head to the EWG's website at www.foodnews.org.

Remember: when you buy organic, you are not only making a commitment to better health, you are also putting your money where your mouth is—by supporting farming methods that are easier on the earth.

Buy These Organic

According to the Environmental Working Group (EWG), these fruits and vegetables have the highest detected pesticide levels:

- Peaches
- Apples
- Sweet bell peppers
- Celery
- Nectarines
- Strawberries
- Grapes (imported)
- Strawberries
- Cherries
- Lettuce
- Potatoes
- Pears
- Spinach

Lowest In Pesticides

The EWG points to these 12 fruits and vegetables as the lowest in pesticides:

- Onions
- Avocados
- Sweet corn (frozen)
- Pineapples
- Mangos
- Sweet peas (frozen)
- Asparagus
- Kiwis
- Bananas
- Cabbage
- Broccoli
- Eggplant

Moving Over to Organic Milk

ONCE YOU'VE VALIANTLY braved your way through the produce section, you are more than ready—and armed with information—to make some positive changes in the milk cooler. Again, pesticides come into play here and they are joined by antibiotics, fertilizers (for growing feed), and hormones. All of these harmful elements are used to streamline dairy farming operations and make the cows produce more milk than their bodies are typically capable of. But, in the end, how safe is our milk?

Cost Meter:

Today, a vast number of dairy cows are injected with recombinant bovine growth hormone (rBGH), a genetically engineered hormone that increases milk production. This hormone, to date, has not passed through any type of safety testing for its long-term health effects. The Canadian government, after reviewing the results of rBGH's effects in animal studies, decided not to approve the hormone for use.

In addition, the Environmental Working Group conducted a study of milk samples that found the presence of pechlorate, the main ingredient in rocket fuel. Some samples found doses that were twice the safe level for consumption. This chemical, which can cause thyroid disorders, is believed to have made its way into milk from runoff created at military plants and bases that flowed into the water supply used by farms.

Because of consumer concern over the presence of these chemicals in milk products—not to mention the inhumane treatment of the animals, which suffer from overcrowded conditions and abnormally swollen and inflamed udders—organic milk has seen a spike in sales over the last few years. In 2005, organic milk and cream sales tipped over the $1 billion mark, up a full 25 percent from 2004. These organic products now account for an estimated 6 percent of all retail milk sales. The USDA's national organic standards prohibit the use of antibiotics and hormones in livestock production and specify that animals must be fed organic feed and be given access to the outdoors.

In 2001, there were over 36,000 certified organic dairy cows in the U.S. ©istockphoto.com/Gordon Dixon

A study conducted by Danish Institute of Agricultural Research also discovered that organic milk is actually higher in beneficial nutrients than conventional milk. Looking at cows farmed both organically and conventionally, the researchers found that the organic cows produced milk that was, on average, 50 percent higher in Vitamin E than standard milk. It also revealed that organic milk was 75 percent higher in beta carotene and two to three times higher in lutein and zeaxanthine, both antioxidants. Higher levels of heart-healthy omega 3 essential fatty acids were also found.

While organic milk also costs slightly more than conventionally produced milk—again, because the farming practices are more costly to farmers—the peace of mind you will receive is well worth the extra amount you'll be padding your milk budget. Milk is probably one of the most important items on which you can spend your organic budget.

What's lurking inside your glass of milk?
©istockphoto.com/imagestock

Buying Green Eggs and Ham

I T WILL COME AS NO SURPRISE, given the state of milk produced from conventionally farmed cows, that meats like beef, chicken, and pork have their own set of issues. Feedlot cows are fed an unnatural diet of soy and corn and they are regularly given antibiotics to promote growth. In addition, they are raised in crowded spaces that can, when mixed with an overabundance of manure, become breeding grounds for bacteria. We have seen the results of this in the appearance of Salmonella and E.coli in our meat supply and even mad cow disease.

Many of these problems are also present in the poultry and pork markets, as well. Chickens are typically raised in extremely crowded spaces and never get to roam outside their entire lives. These areas are typically riddled with bacteria, bugs, and disease, which is why these animals are loaded up with antibiotics, insecticides, and even arsenic, which controls infections. Not only is this treatment inhumane to the animals, its elements slip into our food supply.

Annual global meat production is projected to sky-rocket from 229 million tons in 2000 to 465 million tons in 2050. ©istockphoto.com/Skip ODonnell

Cost Meter:

Some consumers have resolved to add more plant proteins, such as beans and nuts, into their diets to cut down on meat consumption. Even tasty grains, such as quinoa and amaranth, can supply all the protein the body needs. At the same time, organic and other healthier options have evolved in the meat market to deliver a product that is better for the health of our families and the planet. Look for certified organic meats in your grocery or health food store to avoid a potential dose of pathogens and chemicals. This designation means the animals were not given hormones or antibiotics plus they were fed organic feed and given access to the outdoors for grazing.

Other healthy, humane labels to watch for include "Grass Fed" (meaning livestock has continuous access to a natural pasture) and "Free-Farmed," where animals are raised with appropriate space and not fed antibiotics; this designation is monitored and meets standards set up by the American Humane Association. When buying eggs, choose organic, which is a catchall for many of the more positive labels such as "antibiotic-free" and "vegetarian-fed;" organic laying hens also have access to the outdoors.

Be wary of labels like "Natural," "Cage Free," or "Free Range," as these are not verified like "Organic" and "Free-Farmed." Oftentimes, "Cage Free" simply means chickens are out of cages and loose in an indoor space with thousands of other birds.

Fishy Business

THE BENEFITS OF EATING inherently high-protein, low-fat fish are many, including its heart-healthy omega-3-boosting qualities. But, do you know where your fillets are coming from?

Fish farms supply about half the world's demand for fish, but they harbor some disheartening secrets. The lion's share of the seafood Americans eat comes from farms located overseas where their operations are not adequately regulated. Fish are typically kept in very small, crowded spaces, such as concrete tanks or pens.

As you might expect, this environment breeds disease and bacteria. Many fish are also fed unnatural diets that often contain contaminants, drugs, and chemicals. As a result, the fish that ends up on your dinner plate can be host to a number of things you don't want to ingest. A recent study by Wake Forest University found that some farm-raised fish, such as tilapia and catfish, contain an alarmingly high amount of omega-6 fats, which can cause autoimmune diseases, cancer, and osteoporosis. In fact, one serving of tilapia was found to contain more omega-6s than bacon or doughnuts. Researchers believe this is due to the diet the farmed fish are fed. Other independent lab studies have also shown that farmed fish can be high in PCBs, which are pollutants.

This fish farm in Malaysia is part of the aquaculture industry, which is growing at a rate three times faster than land-based animal agriculture.
©istockphoto.com/graham heywood

Aquaculture can also have harmful effects on the environment. Some farms allow food, fish waste, and chemicals to flow into the surrounding waters, which pollutes the oceans and affects the health of wild fish. Additionally, predatory fish like salmon are fed huge amounts of wild fish like mackerel, herring, and anchovies—more pounds of wild fish are consumed than the farms actually produce.

On the wild side, the news is also not inspiring as the world's oceans are increasingly becoming depleted from overfishing. It is currently estimated that 90 percent of species of large predatory fish are gone. A 2006 report in the journal *Science* explained that several of the world's top marine biologists had concluded that if unsustainable fishing practices continued, it could lead to a worldwide crash of all fish and seafood species by 2048.

Adding to the problems is the fact that seafood caught in our oceans tends to have high mercury levels, which we end up consuming when we eat fish and shellfish. As such, the FDA has issued an advisory to pregnant women, women who may become pregnant, nursing mothers, and young children to avoid certain fish altogether, such as shark and swordfish, and to limit consumption of other low-mercury fish (such as shrimp, salmon, and canned light tuna) to 12 ounces per week.

Between 1950 and 1994, ocean fishermen doubled the number of boats in use and employed more efficient fishing gear. The result was an increase in their catch by 400 percent. But, in 1989, the yearly catch of the world's fisherman leveled off at just over 82 million metric tons. Experts say that this amount is all that the ocean is capable of producing, even as our population and food needs continue to grow.

Eco Fact

Did you know that the world's meat-eating habits take a heavy toll on the planet? According to the Food and Agriculture Organization of the United Nations (UN), livestock are responsible for 18 percent of greenhouse gas emissions as measured in carbon dioxide equivalent. In fact, UN figures suggest that meat production emits more greenhouse gases than transportation as a whole. This surprising truth is a result of the deforestation that is taking place to increase pasture and feed crop acreage, the energy used to run processing plants and produce fertilizers, plus the manure and flatulence of grass-guzzling cattle. Sadly, it's no laughing matter—the average American diet is estimated to produce 1.5 tons more of greenhouse gases yearly than a no-meat diet, which is about half the yearly emissions of a small car. Can you eat less meat? Doing so will be a significant contribution to lowering your own carbon footprint.

Buying Safer Seafood

ON THE BRIGHTER SIDE, there is a movement afoot to clean up fish farm operations and to implement more sustainable fishing practices. Organizations like the Environmental Defense Fund (EDF) are hard at work to stave off problems like overfishing, aquaculture mismanagement, and even supply collapse. But, they need our help.

What can you do to help the planet and also put healthy fish on your family's dinner table? Making the right fish choices at the supermarket is the most important step you can take.

One key strategy is to stick to smaller fish, both farmed and wild-caught, because they have less time in the water to absorb toxins. Experts agree that fish at the top of the food chain happen to be higher in contaminants because they have a greater concentration effect from living longer in the water and eating other fish. Smaller fish are also a more sustainable food source.

The EDF (www.edf.org) has developed a list of fish that are both good for you and the environment. Those fish on its "Eco-Best" list include:

▶ Anchovies

▶ Arctic Char (farmed)

▶ Atlantic Mackerel

▶ Mussels

▶ Oysters (farmed)

▶ Sablefish (from Alaska and Canada)

Cost Meter:

▶ Wild Alaskan Salmon

▶ Pacific Sardines (from the U.S.)

▶ Rainbow Trout (farmed)

▶ Albacore Tuna (from the U.S. and Canada)

Those fish on the "Eco-Worst" list include:

▶ Chilean sea bass

▶ Grouper

▶ Monkfish

▶ Orange Roughy

▶ Salmon (farmed/Atlantic)

▶ Shark

▶ Swordfish (imported)

▶ Tilefish (Gulf of Mexico/South Atlantic)

▶ Bigeye and Yellowfin Tuna (imported longline)

▶ Bluefin Tuna

Sushi lovers can also get schooled on the best raw fish choices for both personal health and the planet with the Environmental Defense Fund's Sushi Selector, available at: http://www.edf.org/page.cfm?tagID=29774.

Green Idea

What's in your can? The FDA says that about 17 percent of the American diet comes straight out of cans. But, these cans, which house everything from fish like tuna and salmon to vegetables and fruits, have become a hot topic because many have an epoxy liner made with the notorious chemical Bisphenol A (BPA), which has been linked to heart disease, diabetes, and breast cancer. A test study conducted by the Environmental Working Group found BPA in more than half of all samples at levels the group said were 200 times the safe level of exposure to industrial chemicals set by the government. You can cut back on BPA by purchasing foods in alternative packaging such as Tetra Paks, aseptic cartons made from layers of paper, and glass bottles; some natural foods companies, such as Eden Foods, are also offering products in BPA-free cans.

Buying Locally Grown Food

HOW MANY "FOOD MILES" did the snack you just had or the steak you ate the other night travel to sate your appetite? By definition, "food miles" refers to the distance a food item travels door-to-door from the farm to your fridge or cupboard. In the U.S., grocery store-bought produce is shipped an average of 1,500 miles from the farm where it was produced to reach you.

While about half of our entire country's land space is devoted to farmland, we still ship in about 40 percent of our fruits from overseas. Oftentimes, food products (including meat) are shipped to us from as far away as Australia and New Zealand. A 2003 report from the Leopold Center for Sustainable Agriculture at Iowa State University said that while most Americans live within 60 miles of an apple orchard, this fruit is typically shipped over 1,700 miles to reach our grocery stores.

Cost Meter:

Even though most Americans have tomatoes growing within 60 miles of their home, they are typically shipped over 1,500 miles to our grocery stores.
©istockphoto.com/Michael Krinke

While this is not necessarily bad for your health (although some countries do not regulate the use of chemicals like pesticides, fertilizers, hormones, and antibiotics), the real toll is taken on the planet. An enormous amount of fossil fuels are used to transport our food across these long distances. As you know by now, the burning of these fossil fuels creates emissions that contribute greatly to climate change and air pollution.

Help quell the madness by spending some of your weekly grocery budget at local farms. Typically, local health food stores and some grocers will sell products from local producers.

Or, check out www.localharvest.org, which enables you to enter your zip code and the product you are looking for to find local farm options. Because they are smaller in nature, many of these farms employ sustainable farming practices and humane animal treatment. While some may be certified organic farms, obtaining this certification is costly and time-consuming, so many farms that use earth-friendly methods (i.e., no pesticides, fertilizers, hormones, etc.) may not boast this classification. Since you'll be going directly to the source, you can ask them how they farm their land and livestock. Their method of farming can be more costly than mass production, so buying food locally can be just a little more expensive than in the grocery store.

Shopping at the Farmer's Market

THE BEST AND EASIEST place to scoop up local and organic produce, baked goods, dairy products, and meats is at the farmer's market in your area. Consumers' increasing passion for healthy, organic, and earth-friendly foods has spurred the growth of the farmer's market concept, which is virtually a sustainable, eco-conscious supermarket of freshly harvested and produced foods.

Today, nearly 4,700 farmer's markets are in operation from coast to coast, according to the USDA's Agricultural Marketing Service (AMS). This number represents about a 7 percent increase over the number of markets in 2006 and a whopping 37 percent growth in farmer's markets since 1994.

Cost Meter:

The AMS offers an up-to-date list of all farmer's markets across the country. You can easily find the market closest to you by entering your zip code or county name at http://apps.ams.usda. gove/FarmersMarkets. A market listing by state is also available at www.farmersmarket.com. Depending on where you live, the local farmer's market could be open year-round or at least six months a year in colder climates. Since these farmers are typically using more cost-intensive, sustainable farming practices, the food you buy here may be slightly more expensive than the same non-organic options at the grocery store.

Most farmer's markets feature items from farms within the local region. For example, the Union Square Greenmarket in New York City offers food produced within 170 miles of Manhattan, underscoring the fact that local, organic foods are attainable even in urban areas. Each market typically carries a wide variety of produce that is in season at the time you shop there. In the spring, it may be everything from strawberries to lettuce. In the summer, you can indulge in sweet peaches, ripe tomatoes, and juicy melons. In the fall, you'll find tasty foods ranging from apples and pears to butternut squash.

Many farmer's markets also feature stands of fresh, cut flowers from local farms.

Eco Fact

Each year, more than one million acres of land in the U.S. is lost to business and residential development. Each acre given up to development is an acre that will never be used to help feed our fast-growing population.

There is never a lack of selection and you can enjoy the fact that you are reducing carbon emissions by buying straight from the source. Supporting the local farmers in your area is also a way of infusing your money right back into the community in which you live instead of into the pockets of middlemen, shippers, and farmers in different countries. Eating local is also a path to restoring integrity in our food system and helping to build a more sustainable society.

Nature's bounty is right around the corner at your local farmer's market.
©istockphoto.com/Christopher Hudson

Drinking Clean Water

TODAY, CLEAN WATER IS A rarity—even what pours out of our taps can be expected to contain small amounts of contaminants. According to the EPA, some studies have even shown that pharmaceuticals like antibiotics are present in some of our nation's water bodies, including drinking water sources. And, after analyzing data on the presence of arsenic in drinking water in 25 states, the Natural Resources Defense Council (NRDC) determined that "more than 34 million Americans drink tap water supplied by systems containing average levels of arsenic that pose unacceptable cancer risks." Lead is also a cause for concern as it is a common contaminant in our water supply and is especially dangerous for pregnant women and small children.

To ensure you're drinking clean water, install a water filter and maintain it regularly.
©istockphoto.com/Ina Peters

Cost Meter: **$** to **$$**

While most healthy adults can drink tap water without issue, according to the NRDC, some groups are more vulnerable, including the elderly, young children, pregnant women, and people with autoimmune disorders. The causes of the contamination of concern include pollution, old pipes, and outdated treatment systems. According to the Denver Water 2008 Water Quality Report, the culprits in our water can include:

▶ **Microbial Contaminants** like viruses and bacteria that come from sewage treatment plants, septic systems, and agricultural livestock operations.

▶ **Inorganic Contaminants** like salts and metals, which occur from storm water runoff, oil and gas production, and mining.

▶ **Pesticides and Herbicides** used in agricultural and residential applications.

▶ **Organic Chemical Contaminants** including synthetic and volatile organic chemicals that come from industrial production, gas stations, and septic systems.

▶ **Radioactive Contaminants** that are naturally occurring or a result of mining, plus oil and gas production.

Eco Fact

If you're thinking bottled water is the answer, think again—the Environmental Working Group recently conducted a study that found bottled water to contain an array of contaminants, including fertilizers, pain medication, and disinfection byproducts. Additionally, plastic water bottles that are not recycled simply add to the country's overflowing landfill problems.

Most likely, you can find out what's in your water by contacting your water utility company and asking for their annual quality report. You can also access some reports online through the EPA's website at www.epa.gov/safewater/dwinfo/index.html. Testing for lead is also a good idea, since this can vary from home to home—lead test kits cost about $25 and are available at www.leadtesting.org.

Once you determine your water's hidden content, you can address the problem by installing a water filter in your home. Point-of-entry filters, which treat water before it is distributed throughout your house's water systems, are an excellent choice but can be costly and labor-intensive to install.

A faster and more cost-effective (but still efficient) solution is to install a point-of-use unit—the options include filtered pitchers (such as those offered by Brita), faucet filters, and under-the-sink units. These can vary in price from $12 for a filtered pitcher to $25 for a faucet filter. Whatever filter you choose, make sure its label indicates it meets NSF/ANSI standard 53 and is certified to remove the specific contaminants of concern in your own water.

In most cases, a simple activated carbon filter will get the job done on most pollutants. An informative comparison chart can be viewed at www.waterfiltercomparisons.com. If you have unique contaminants, such as perchlorate, heavy metals, parasites like Giardia, or bacteria, check out the NRDC's filter guide at www.nrdc.org/water/drinking/gfilters.asp. A range of filter options will be available at your local hardware or home improvement store.

Green on the Cheap

Choose to Re-Use: Continue your eco-consciousness on the go by toting a reusable water bottle ($5 to $15) in lieu of consuming water from costly, disposable water bottles. Once you've set up a water filtration system at home, what comes out of your tap (or filtered pitcher) will probably be some of the cleanest water you can drink. And, since Americans drink more than seven billion gallons of bottled water a year and 77 percent of all those plastic bottles are not recycled, your choice will do the planet a whole lot of good. Just be sure your bottle is BPA-free; choose stainless steel or a plastic bottle that is clearly marked as BPA-free.

The Fresco reusable aluminum bottle from Bilt offers a functional way to carry water in a well-designed, BPA-free, earth-friendly package. ©Bilt

Green Review:
Changes to Focus on During Week Three

1. Add some organic foods into your cart during the week's shopping trip. Best bets for avoiding pesticides include peaches, apples, sweet bell peppers, celery, nectarines, and strawberries.

2. Swap out regular milk for organic next time you visit the dairy department.

3. Toss "organic," "grass fed," or "free farmed" beef or chicken into your cart, along with a package of "organic" eggs.

4. When shopping for seafood, focus on healthy, eco-conscious choices like farmed Arctic Char, mussels, wild Alaskan salmon, farmed rainbow trout, and Albacore Tuna (from the U.S. and Canada).

5. Ask your grocery or natural foods store clerk or manager if they stock any locally produced produce or meats. Or, do a web search for local farms at www.localharvest.org.

6. If in season, locate your area's farmer's market via www.farmersmarket.com and opt to do part of your weekly shopping here instead of the grocery store.

7. Purchase some type of water filtration system for your home; simple, inexpensive filtered pitcher versions are available from www.Brita.com.

©istockphoto.com/Andrejs Zemdega

TrueGreen: Joining a CSA

IF YOU ARE INCLINED TO travel just a bit further along your green cuisine journey, one of the next steps could be to join a CSA. This acronym stands for Community Supported Agriculture and its definition is just that—a community of individuals that each pledges a set amount of money to support a local farm for the growing season.

As a "member" or "shareholder," you would help cover the farmer's anticipated costs of operation and take stock, in essence, of the upcoming crop. This includes the risks of a weather-affected growing season as well as the potential rewards of a bountiful harvest.

When you join a community-supported agriculture program, you get a weekly box of fresh produce.
©istockphoto.com/Georgina Palmer

In return, CSA members typically receive a large box or bag of fresh produce on a weekly basis from the farm. Many CSAs offer different share sizes (i.e., "small" for one to two people or "large" for a big family). The range can include everything from Swiss chard and tomatoes to strawberries, melons, and turnips, depending on the time of year. There is perhaps no better illustration of the flow of the growing seasons—and the changing variety of produce produced during this time—than the contents of a CSA box. As such, many CSAs serve up lists of recipes with each box to help you discover new ways to eat the foods they deliver.

Some CSAs, especially those in metro areas, do offer delivery service to your door. Others designate a weekly day, time, and place for pickup. Most CSA seasons run from late spring through early fall, ranging from a start in May or June and a finish in September or October.

When you support a CSA, you are helping to keep food dollars in the local community and build regional food production. You are also supporting your local farmer, who can focus less on marketing and sales and more on growing quality crops. Since most local farms employ sustainable farming practices, you are also supporting the planet and putting your money into food grown with integrity.

You can search for Community Supported Agriculture programs in your own area at http://www.localharvest.org/csa.

SuperGreen: Take the Challenge

DO YOU ASPIRE TO be a locavore? Take your earth-friendly inclinations even one step further and go SuperGreen by signing up for a challenge to eat more local foods. Check out www.eatlocalchallenge.com, which is a blog about people who have committed to eat more local foods. Or, sign up for the Eat Local America Challenge, sponsored by the National Cooperative Grocers Association (NCGA). Joining in either of these unique challenges is a fun way to learn how to eat more local foods.

Green Idea

How much does a CSA cost? Prices can vary widely depending on your location, the share size, and mode of delivery, but most range between $250 and $450 for a full season. In 2002, researchers at Iowa State University set out to determine how the cost of a CSA stacked up against buying the same organic produce at the grocery store. They found over the course of the CSA delivery season that the same amounts of produce at retail grocery prices would have cost over $560.

The Eat Local America Challenge invites individuals to try to consume 80 percent of their diets from food that has been grown or produced locally—that's four out of every five meals. This is no simple feat, but to make your charge simple, the Challenge runs in the summer during the peak harvest times for your region's growing season. For example, the 2008 Challenge ran from June 15th to July 15th in the South, Southwest, and California and from July 15th to August 15th in the Plains, Midwest, and Northwest. In the Northeast, Mid-Atlantic, Ohio Valley, and Upper Midwest, it ran from August 15th through December 15th. The Challenge asks participants, depending on their location, to focus on foods grown within a 200- to 500-mile radius of their home.

The Challenge is hosted locally by NCGA member stores, which are retail food co-ops that have traditionally had a strong focus on natural, organic, and local foods. Co-ops typically offer discounts on grocery items for those who buy a membership, but those without memberships can still shop at most stores.

There are over 130 participating NCGA stores in 32 states, but aspiring locavores can also sign up for the Eat Local America Challenge on the web at www.eatlocalamerica.com. It is a test of willpower and perseverance, no doubt. Put thoughts of fast foods aside and be prepared to spend some time shopping and cooking. Serving up this much local food is a slow but incredibly worthwhile endeavor.

Green Idea

What is a locavore? This new word, which was named the 2007 Word of the Year for the Oxford American Dictionary, defines a person who is part of the "locavore" movement. According to the Oxford American Dictionary, this movement "encourages consumers to buy from farmers' markets or even to grow or pick their own food, arguing that fresh, local products are more nutritious and taste better. Locavores also shun supermarket offerings as an environmentally friendly measure, since shipping food over long distances often requires more fuel for transportation."

Eating local foods helps reduce greenhouse gases and eases the strain on the planet.
©istockphoto.com/Valentin Casarsa

Is your yard green *and* clean? ©istockphoto.com/PhotographerOlympus

Week Four:
Green Your Yard

6

D O YOU HAVE—or aspire to have—the perfect lawn that is deeply
green, neatly trimmed, with every blade in order? It would
certainly be a splendid spot to rest and relax or play and picnic.

Or, perhaps your passion lies in the garden, where the plants thrive, the
flowers bloom, and the vegetables grow. It is a place that provides a
tranquil hideaway, a sense of accomplishment, and a gathering spot for
backyard animals, birds, and butterflies. Ah, the idyllic American yard.

Some perfectly groomed yards are the result of hours of labor or the
paid handiwork of a gardener or lawn care specialist. Many are given a
boost by organic or inorganic fertilizers. Most require a vast amount of
water to stay in business.

These realities are what make the majority of lawns an endeavor that
is anything but earth-friendly. Fertilizers, pesticides, and herbicides can
contain toxic chemicals that can negatively affect the health of your
children, your pets, yourself, and even the purity of your water supply.
They can also ultimately disrupt the balance and future sustainability
of the world's ecosystems. Additionally, water use for landscaping can
be a major suck on the earth's clean-water resources. It is estimated
that landscape irrigation in the U.S. totals more than seven billion
gallons of water per day.

This chapter will show you how to make your yard a more earth-friendly
and health-conscious place, all while maintaining its beauty—and saving
you some money.

The Problem with Fertilizers, Herbicides, and Pesticides

THE DRAW OF THE AMERICAN dream lawn lies in its tidy perfection. But, the quest for this ideal has led to a dependence on the fertilizers, herbicides (weed killers), and pesticides that help keep it all so neat, green, and uniform. Unfortunately, often unbeknownst to homeowners, these chemical blends can contain ingredients that are harmful to both their families and the planet.

While we already know that some of the ingredients in fertilizers and pesticides aren't doing our farms any favors, it turns out that the problem is even more prolific when it comes to our residences. The National Academy of Sciences estimates that homeowners use approximately ten times more chemical fertilizers and pesticides per acre than is used on the country's farmland.

A worker applies a chemical lawn treatment.
©istockphoto.com/Marcel Pelletier

This equates to quite a bit, since over 30 million acres are planted in residential lawns across the country. North Americans take their lawns seriously; they spent a combined $40 billion on lawn care in 2005. Most of this rings in as sales of pesticides, herbicides, and fertilizers. Well over 70 million pounds of pesticides are applied on lawns, gardens, and shrubs yearly and over $5 billion is spent annually on non-organic fertilizers that are derived from unsustainable fossil fuels.

Conventional fertilizers and pesticides are concocted using an array of minerals and chemicals, most of which are quite effective in increasing the growth rate of the plant life in your yard. But, some of these ingredients are possible carcinogens that can be harmful to people (especially children), animals, and the planet.

For instance, 2,4-D is one of the world's most common herbicides used to control weeds, yet long-term exposure has been tied to liver, kidney, and nervous system damage. Its chemical name may not be familiar to you as it is sold under a variety of popular brand names—it was also the main ingredient in Agent Orange.

The Environmental Protection Agency (EPA) estimates that Americans use nine million pounds of 2,4-D a year to control lawn and garden weeds. While the EPA has placed no limitations on the use of 2,4-D, the World Health Organization's International Agency for Research on Cancer has classified it as a possible human carcinogen and its use has been banned in a number of countries including Sweden, Kuwait, and Norway.

On the pesticide front, one of the most commonly used is glyphosate, which is also marketed under other brand names. It is estimated that Americans make 25 million applications per year of this pesticide. While glyphosate is only considered to be "mildly toxic," it is still reported to cause skin and eye irritation plus lung congestion and an increased breathing rate. In the long-term, it can cause liver and kidney damage plus reproductive effects. Because of these issues, the EPA has set standards for the presence of glyphosate in our drinking water.

How does a pesticide make its way into our drinking water? While your intention may purely be to create a beautiful lawn and garden for all to enjoy, the chemicals you use there can harm those who come into contact with them in the yard, plus even those who do not. Pesticides, herbicides, and fertilizers can make their way into our homes (and those of others) on shoes and they also have a tendency to drift via air and even enter groundwater, streams, and rivers when they're washed away in a rainstorm. In the end, they make their way into our water supply.

As you can see, employing these products contributes to environmental issues that reach far beyond your own home. They can also impact pets and wildlife more severely, due to their smaller systems. A 2004 study conducted by scientists at Purdue University found that Scottish Terriers were four to seven times more likely to develop bladder cancer if they had been exposed to lawn chemicals. It is also estimated that lawn-care pesticides kill approximately seven million birds in the U.S. each year.

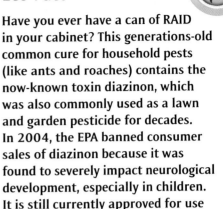

Eco Fact

Have you ever have a can of RAID in your cabinet? This generations-old common cure for household pests (like ants and roaches) contains the now-known toxin diazinon, which was also commonly used as a lawn and garden pesticide for decades. In 2004, the EPA banned consumer sales of diazinon because it was found to severely impact neurological development, especially in children. It is still currently approved for use in agricultural application, but is slowly being phased out.

Lastly, a 2001 report by CALPIRG, California's largest environmental, consumer, and good government advocacy group, found that the recycling of hazardous industrial wastes into fertilizers was sending toxic metals like lead and mercury into our lawns and gardens. From 1990 to 1995, the steel industry alone sent fertilizer companies over 80 million pounds of waste because of its high zinc content, which is an essential nutrient for plant growth. However, this waste can also include arsenic, cadmium, nickel, and dioxin, all highly toxic substances. The CALPIRG report found that 29 tested fertilizers contained 22 toxic heavy metals that have been linked to human health hazards. Because fertilizer labels lack critical information on ingredients—most states only require beneficial ingredients to be listed on packages—consumers are left in the dark when it comes to determining what's best for their health, their homes, and the planet.

Using Sustainable Lawn and Garden Practices

ITCH THE FERTILIZERS, pesticides, and herbicides in your life and truly "green" your yard by putting a few simple and natural lawn and garden care strategies into play. Knowing your outdoor space is safe and healthy for your family, your pets, and the local ecosystems will bring a whole new sense of accomplishment to your gardening endeavors. Whether you are starting to plan for the growing season ahead or are in the thick of it, these simple steps will ensure that your yard is eco-friendly.

Is your lawn safe for consumption?
©istockphoto.com/druvo

Eco Fact

Do you need a wheelbarrow full of chemicals to have a green, attractive lawn? New York City says "No." In 2003, the New York City Department of Parks & Recreation won an award from the EPA for excellent environmental stewardship of its nearly 29,000 acres of open space—it greatly scaled back on the use of pesticides and fertilizers plus it widely employed the practice of non-chemical pest management techniques. In Central Park, the application of insecticides dropped from 220 pounds in 2001 to a mere 45 pounds in 2003. At the same time, herbicide use decreased from 70 pounds in 2000 to only 7.5 pounds in 2003. Instead, the Department of Parks & Recreation relied on organic fertilizers plus organic, non-toxic pest control products, including one made from corn gluten.

Building Strong Soil

YOU CAN REPLACE THE need for conventional fertilizers by going straight to the source and pumping up the nutrients in your soil—naturally. Every lawn and garden benefits from its soil's proper balance of nitrogen, phosphorous, and potassium, all essential nutrients for plant growth. Your soil may not even need an external boost to deliver healthy plants, flowers, and grass.

The first step to greening your yard is to conduct a soil test to determine exactly what it is that you may or may not need. Your local Cooperative Extension office, a government-funded educational service that you can locate through your area's phone book, and most garden-supply centers stock these inexpensive tests. The best range for your soil pH is between 5.5 and 7.0; if absolutely necessary, you can apply lime to raise the pH or sulfur to lower it.

Cost Meter: **$ $**
(over time, this change will save you money)

The presence of organic matter in your soil is also critical for healthy plant growth. If your soil test reveals that you have less than 5 percent organic matter, buy bags of compost (preferably organic for growing fruits and vegetables) and dig or rototill one to three inches of compost into the top six to twelve inches of topsoil when you're setting up new garden beds or lawns. On existing lawns, lay down about one-quarter to one-half of an inch right on top of lawns in the spring or fall. This new layer will mix in within a matter of days and provide a much healthier environment in which your lawn can thrive.

If you feel you need fertilizer to give a leg up to your annuals, lawn, or vegetable garden, the EPA suggests opting for products that contain "natural organic" or "slow-release" ingredients. The latter significantly reduces runoff into ground and surface waters. These products can be found at most home and garden supply stores or on the Internet at gardening websites like www.planetnatural.com. You'll be amazed at the wealth of natural products—from Epsom salts to corn gluten meal—that are available to help your lawn and garden grow.

Rich soil with the proper pH balance is attainable with organic, natural methods.
©istockphoto.com/Don Nichols

Using Holistic Pest Management

HOME GARDENERS CAN ALSO replace the need for conventional, chemical-derived pesticides by taking a more natural tack with pest management. According to the EPA's Greenscapes program, ongoing pest problems can be an indicator that your lawn and/or garden is not getting what it needs to be the best that it can be. In this case, prevention really can be worth a pound of cure (in pesticides, that is). Greenscapes recommends the following preventative measures:

► Select pest-resistant plants and give them a home in soil and sun/shade conditions they prefer.

► Use a variety of plants so the entire garden is not at risk if pests descend upon it.

► Remove dead plants to eliminate hiding places for insect pests.

All gardens and lawns are home to a certain number of insect pest species, many of which are "good" bugs that actually help control the real pests. Greenscapes estimates that only about 5 to 15 percent of the bugs in your yard are those to be concerned about. If they're not doing any harm, a little tolerance for insects will go a long way in helping to keep pesticides from harming both people and the planet.

Cost Meter: **$** to **$$**
(over time, this change will save you money)

If you find you have a persistent problem, there are natural measures you can take to rid your garden or lawn from the persistence of pests. The first step is to identify the problem. Which pest are you battling? With this knowledge, you can research the proper solution. Physical controls like traps, barriers, fabric row covers, or plants that actually repel pests are your first line of defense. You can also utilize natural alternatives to the chemical pesticides on the market, many of which are sold at home and garden supply shops. Some also stock "beneficial" predator insects, such as the green lacewing and spined soldier bug, which can be released to control the source of your problems.

Chemical-free insect pest management is a beautiful thing. ©istockphoto.com/LyaC

Employing Natural Weed Control

COMPLETE YOUR TOXIN-FREE lawn and garden transformation by getting rid of the conventional herbicides (weed killers) in your life. Are you a lawn and garden perfectionist? A little bit of tolerance is one of the best steps you can take in the quest to go green in your home's outdoor space. A lawn that consists of 15 percent weeds still appears weed-free to the average onlooker.

Catching weeds before they go to seed will reduce your aggravation. ©istockphoto.com/narvikk

Cost Meter: $ to $$
(over time, this change will save you money)

If weed reduction—or elimination—is ingrained into your gardening repertoire, know that there are also effective, natural ways to deal with the problem. While some weeds can be pulled out by hand (and many tools are available for this labor of love), there is also an array of organic and natural herbicides on the market today that can make the job fast and easy—these are available at garden supply stores and websites like www.planetnatural.com.

Green Idea

Did you know that some weeds are actually beneficial to your lawn and garden? The dreaded dandelion provides food for miniscule parasitic wasps that feed on a number of garden pests and white clover even releases nitrogen, which is beneficial to grass. This interplay is an excellent example of how Mother Nature does her job to maintain a sustainable planet. When we add chemicals into the mix, we risk disrupting the flow of nature and endangering the planet's ecosystems.

For an even quicker and less expensive fix, gardeners can look to some items they may have around the home to work as efficient weed killers. The steps you can take with these simple items will save you untold amounts of money in the fertilizer aisle. The Children's Health Environmental Coalition recommends the following herbicide-free methods for eliminating unwanted weeds:

▶ **Boiling Water:** Dousing weeds with boiling water not only rids you of the perpetrator, it also kills weed seeds.

▶ **Soap:** Mix five tablespoons of a household liquid soap, such as dishwashing liquid or hand soap, with one quart of water in a spray bottle and coat weeds with the soapy blend. (Hint: This method works best on hot days.)

▶ **Vinegar:** Pour some regular household vinegar into a spray bottle and douse weeds with this potent product. The makeup of vinegar consists of 5 percent acetic acid in water, so it effectively burns weeds, particularly on sunny days. For an extra-strength spray, do the same with pickling vinegar, which is 9 percent acid. Take care to not get this spray on your other garden plants.

▶ **Alcohol:** If you've got alcohol like vodka or gin in the house, mix up one to five tablespoons (depending on desired potency level) with one quart of water in a spray bottle and spray it on weeds, being careful to keep this blend off your other plants as well.

▶ **Corn Meal Gluten:** If you have the pleasure of seeing your weeds go to seed, you can reduce the damage done by spreading corn meal gluten in the affected area before the seeds sprout. It will not kill existing weeds or plants. Once the corn meal has done its job by ceasing seed germination and rooting, it will politely break down into nitrogen to provide a natural fertilizer for your plants and lawn.

Green Idea

What on earth is xeriscaping? The word was coined by combining the Greek word *xeros*, meaning "dry," with the word "landscaping." This moniker is on target, as xeriscaping is the practice of landscaping in ways that do not require supplemental irrigation. As climate patterns shift and water becomes increasingly scarce, this lawn and garden strategy is gaining popularity. It employs plants whose water needs are appropriate to the particular climate in which they grow. In xeriscaping, care is also taken to reduce the amount of evaporation and runoff incurred during watering. In fact, this practice can reduce landscape water use by as much as 50 to 70 percent.

Water Use in the Yard

THE AMOUNT OF WATER USED across the country on lawns and gardens is truly prolific. The lawn watering habits of Americans on the East Coast account for over 30 percent of all residential water consumption. On the West Coast, this number skyrockets to 60 percent. It's no wonder—a standard lawn sprinkler can use more water in one hour than a combination of 10 toilet flushes, two dishwasher loads, two five-minute showers, plus a full load of laundry.

The great, plush American lawn is founded in large part on water, which just happens to be one of our country's (and the world's) waning resources. In fact, a recent government survey revealed that at least 36 U.S. states are anticipating local, regional, or statewide water shortages by 2013.

It is estimated that keeping a standard American lawn green takes an average of one to two inches of water a week, which equates to over 10,000 gallons. As a result, diminishing water supplies have prompted several areas across the country to place bans on lawn watering and restrictions on planting. In Las Vegas, for example, new homes are limited to 50 percent turf in their front yards. Additionally, the Southern Nevada Water Authority now offers rebates to consumers who rip out their lawns.

But, according to the EPA, the cause of most common plant problems is watering them too much (or too little). You can deepen the color of your green thumb by learning the right amount of water to dole out to your outdoor spaces and conserving this precious resource. In the end, you can feel good about your yard as well as the savings you've realized on your water bill. You will have also cut down on any potential pesticide or fertilizer runoff (which can be caused by over-watering) reaching our ground and surface water. The next page offers a number of tips to get the job done right in an eco-friendly way.

Even the best soil can't absorb the 130 to 260 gallons of water that the average home sprinkler sprays in an hour. ©istockphoto.com/Bradley Mason

Conserving Water

GOING GREEN IN YOUR YARD will also save you some green at the same time. Proper irrigation in your lawn and garden could lead to a 30 to 80 percent savings in your own residential water use—and the same amount of savings for your monthly water bill. The following simple, low-cost steps will help you realize this green goal:

▶ **Water your lawn deeply and infrequently:** Allow the water to soak in and completely dry out before you water again. Deep, infrequent watering is most beneficial for your soil. To reduce evaporation, water in the early morning. If you water at mid-day, much of the water just evaporates. Evening waterings can encourage mold growth and plant disease.

▶ **Keep water off hardscapes:** If water is falling on driveways or patios in addition to the lawn and garden while your sprinkler is in action, it's time to adjust the system. Try to move the sprinkler to a spot—or adjust the heads—so this won't continue to happen. In some cases, it may require replacing sprinklers or heads to do a more efficient job.

Cost Meter: $0
(this change will save you money)

▶ **Choose low-maintenance plants:** Whether you're landscaping an entire yard or simply adding in a few new plants for the season, look to low-water plants that will help save on water use and expense. Choose native and drought-tolerant species that require little water or fertilizer since they are already adapted to the local soil. This choice also protects the natural biodiversity and ecosystems of your area. Your local nursery or garden-supply store will be able to direct you to the best plants for your area.

▶ **Use soaker hoses:** If you're in the market for a new hose, choose soaker hoses instead of sprinklers. A low pressure, soaker system slowly drips irrigation on garden beds and saves up to 50 percent or more of the water put out by sprinklers.

▶ **Put compost and mulch to use:** Compost serves a multitude of garden needs. In addition to providing essential nutrients to soil, it helps soil to hold water in and reduce evaporation. Mulch performs similar duties.

Green Review:
Changes to Focus on During Week Four

1. Conduct a soil test to determine exactly which, if any, nutrients your lawn and garden may need; these inexpensive tests are available through your local Cooperative Extension office and most garden supply centers.

2. If your soil needs a boost, pump it up with bagged compost or choose to use organic and natural fertilizers.

3. Employ preventative pest management solutions such as selecting pest-resistant plants, using a variety of plants, and removing dead plants from your garden. If insect pests become problematic, choose organic and natural pesticides.

4. Try natural weeding methods like hand pulling or organic, natural weed killers. Or, utilize simple, low-cost household items like dishwashing soap, vinegar, alcohol, boiling water, or corn meal gluten.

5. Conserve water in your lawn and garden by:

   - **Watering deeply and infrequently.**
   - **Keeping water off hardscapes.**
   - **Choosing low-maintenance, low-water plants.**
   - **Using soaker hoses instead of sprinklers.**
   - **Placing compost and/or mulch in your garden to help soil hold water and eliminate evaporation.**

©istockphoto.com/Florea Marius

TrueGreen: Learning to Compost

I F YOU'RE CURIOUS ABOUT taking your greening to the next level, consider composting, which is a simple process that turns your everyday trash into gardening gold. All the non-dairy and non-meat food scraps you toss in the trash, along with your outdoor leftovers like leaves, can actually be composted into rich, nutrient-packed compost that acts as the best fertilizer that nature can provide for your lawn and garden.

How does it work? As your waste decomposes, bacteria breaks down the organic materials into compost.

In addition to benefiting our outdoor spaces, composting also helps keep vast amounts of waste out of landfills and, in essence, reduces harmful emissions that occur in the form of landfill gas. Today, yard trimmings and food residuals account for 23 percent of the waste stream in the U.S. There is no question that composting is a winning strategy for the earth and our own backyards. As a testament to the effectiveness and popularity of this trash recycling, emissions-reducing effort, the composting industry (which sells bagged compost) quadrupled in size from 1988 to 2000.

The first step to composting in your backyard is to select a level area that is about three by five feet and located near a water source. Make sure this spot is away from the places where children might play and also out of direct sunlight. Once you've cleared the area from any debris or grass, you're ready to set up a compost bin.

An open space, a compost bin, and garden tools are all you need to get started. ©istockphoto.com/Sebastien Cote

These bins are typically available at garden and home supply stores, online at sites like www.compostbins.com, and oftentimes through your local area's composting program. State-by-state information is available at www.epa.gov/epawaste/conserve/rrr/composting/live.htm. Some people also choose to build their own compost bins out of wood scraps or concrete blocks.

Simply place your food scraps and lawn waste in the bin, making sure that larger items are chopped up. Composting has three basic requirements—brown materials like dead leaves, branches, and twigs; green materials like vegetable waste, grass clippings, and fruit scraps; and water. Moisten all dry materials with water as you add them.

The NatureMill makes composting accessible to everyone, even apartment dwellers. ©NatureMill

Once your compost pile is established, be sure to bury fruit and vegetable waste under 10 inches of compost as you add them. Grass and green waste materials should be mixed into the compost.

You will need to turn the compost pile in the bin every few weeks with a pitchfork or shovel to keep air and moisture evenly distributed. Some bins are actually sold with turning mechanisms. In dry weather, be sure to sprinkle water on the pile to keep it moist. Most bins provide the proper space for air to circulate and secure doors to keep rodents and wildlife at bay.

Your compost will be ready to use within a few months. When the material located at the bottom of the bin is rich and dark in color, your compost is ready to be put to use.

Green Idea

What is vermicomposting? This practice employs the services of worms, which create compost as an end product as they break down the organic matter in your compost pile. Red wigglers, available online and at garden supply stores, are the best invertebrates for the job.

TrueGreen: Which Items Can You Compost?

IF YOU DECIDE THAT COMPOSTING is for you, taking a little time to learn which items you can and cannot compost will save you from any headaches down the road. Some items can contain or release substances that are harmful to the plants on which you use the compost. Others can create odor problems that attract pests like rodents and flies. And a few things, such as pet waste and used cat litter, might contain parasites, bacteria, and viruses that are harmful to humans. It's also important to keep out any yard trimmings that have been treated with chemical pesticides, as this component can kill beneficial composting organisms.

Which city composts the most? San Francisco, where residents send more than 300 tons of compostable waste to local facilities every day.
©istockphoto.com/Sebastien Cote

What to Compost

▶ **Fruits and vegetables**

▶ **Eggshells**

▶ **Nut shells**

▶ **Tea bags**

▶ **Coffee grounds and filters**

▶ **Clean paper**

▶ **Fireplace ashes**

▶ **Leaves**

▶ **Yard trimmings**

▶ **Dryer and vacuum cleaner lint**

▶ **Cotton and wool rags**

▶ **Cardboard rolls**

What NOT to Compost

▶ **Dairy products (i.e., butter, milk, yogurt, egg yolks, sour cream)**

▶ **Fats, lard, grease, or oils**

▶ **Meat or fish scraps and bones**

▶ **Coal or charcoal ash**

▶ **Diseased or insect-infested plants**

▶ **Pet waste**

▶ **Yard trimmings treated with chemical pesticides**

▶ **Black walnut tree leaves or twigs**

—Information courtesy EPA

Green Idea

Whether you simply just don't have the outdoor space for a compost bin or you prefer not to have this item in your backyard, there is a new option just for you. The NatureMill indoor composter (the first of its kind) enables you to add waste items—even dairy, meat, and fish—at any time of day. It can process up to 120 pounds of waste a month. An upper chamber mixes, heats, and aerates the waste (which is combined with a small amount of sawdust and baking soda) into compost, which will later transfer to the lower chamber. Every two weeks, a container of compost will be ready for your use in the garden or for household plants. At $299 to $399, this item is not inexpensive, but your compost just may pay for itself over time as you replace chemical fertilizers and store-bought compost with homemade, all-natural compost.

SuperGreen:
Converting to a Push or Electric Mower

DOES YOU LAWN MOWER burn fossil fuels? When it's ready to be retired or you're ready to make a switch, you can take your green inclinations even one step further by joining the push and electric lawn mower revolution.

In 2007 alone, it is estimated that six million gas-powered, walk-behind mowers hit the market for sale. But, according to the EPA, the average homeowner's gas lawn mower spits out as much pollution per hour as 11 automobiles during the same time. If just half of all U.S. gas mowers were replaced by their electric counterparts, it would be the emissions equivalent of taking two million cars off the road.

Choose to push it—you'll save a massive amount of pollution from wafting into the air.
©istockphoto.com/Brian Carpenter

For those who would enjoy the exercise, a push mower can eliminate carbon emissions (except for those you breathe out) and replace a trip to the gym (where, if you're using electric-powered exercise machines, you're likely also burning fossil fuels). In fact, in one hour of push mowing, a 165-pound person will burn over 500 calories. Due to the green movement, push mowers are enjoying a renaissance, with approximately 350,000 sold currently in the U.S. each year. This number is a significant jump over the 50,000 sold per year in the 1980s. The cost of entry is comparatively low—most efficient push mowers range from $100 to $200.

Pushing a mower burns about 500 calories per hour.
©istockphoto.com/Sonja Fagnan

Green Idea

A few easy and low-cost natural gardening strategies:

- **Rake Your Lawn:** Thatch, which is the layer of decomposing plant material that naturally develops between the grass blades and soil, can build up if your lawn is not raked to rid it of leaves. Thatch can also prevent water and nutrients from penetrating the soil.

- **Mow High:** When you mow, try to cut only one-third of the height of the grass; this practice enables taller grass to prevent weeds from getting sun and water. Also, leave your grass clippings—they add essential nutrients to the soil and save money on fertilizers (it has been estimated this act is comparable to one fertilizer application).

- **Aerate Your Lawn:** Aerating will deliver what grass needs, since its roots need air to circulate around them and water to penetrate the soil surface. You can rent an aerating machine or hire a professional to perform this job, which could reveal a healthier, greener lawn.

Green on the Cheap

How do you know how much to water your lawn and garden? The EPA suggests scattering clean, empty tuna cans or other solid containers on your lawn and garden before watering. Turn on the sprinkler, check the time, and watch the level of water in the cans. Once they have about an inch of water in them, turn off the sprinkler and check the time. This test will reveal just how long you should leave your sprinklers on each week in the summer to keep your outdoor space green and healthy. You can really make a difference by purchasing a sprinkler timer. This handy and relatively inexpensive device will make your watering easy and perfectly timed and will help conserve gallons of water.

The purchase of an electric mower bumps up the price tag to several hundred dollars, but this quiet, easy-to-use, emissions-reducing machine will only cost about five dollars a year for its fuel—electricity. Electric lawn mowers offer the convenience and effectiveness of a gas-powered machine without all the pollution, noise, and expense. Older models of electric mowers feature long electrical cords, but newer versions are cordless and run off batteries installed internally. Mowing with electricity is an especially green activity if you have purchased renewable energy credits for your home's energy use.

Electric mowers are a green choice for homeowners with larger lawn areas—today, they come in cordless options. ©istockphoto.com/mark noak

How green is your clothing? ©istockphoto.com/Joshua Blake

Week Five:
Green Your Wardrobe

WHETHER YOU VIEW IT AS UTILITARIAN and functional or a creative expression of your own individual style, clothing is a necessity for most Americans. It also happens to be big business. According to the NPD Group, sales of apparel in 2007 were nearly $200 billion, a number that continues to grow over the years, including a 3 percent jump in sales since 2006.

Who is spending all this cash for clothing? Women's apparel accounted for just over half of the clothing sold last year, while men's duds rang in less than 30 percent of sales. Sales of kids' clothing came in closely behind at just under 20 percent of all apparel sold in the U.S.

While pants, dresses, shirts, and shoes may look innocent enough hanging blithely on store hangers or sitting on displays, the apparel industry also lays claim to some environmentally unsound and unhealthy practices. Everything from genetically modified fibers and cancer-causing chemicals to petroleum-based products and disposal issues brings up a number of questions about the sustainability of what we wear on a daily basis.

How eco-friendly are the fabrics that spend the day next to our skin? Do they harbor unseen health risks? Was that shirt manufactured in a responsible way? What is the carbon footprint of those shoes? How much of our unwanted clothing ends up in landfills?

Because apparel is such an important aspect of our culture and it commands a significant amount of Americans' disposable incomes, its journey from plant to fiber to store rack also has a significant impact on the earth.

In this chapter, we'll look at the problems associated with apparel as well as the innovative solutions and style-driven, eco-conscious designs this industry is delivering at a time when the public—and the planet—need them most.

Pesticides Aren't Just for Food Crops

COTTON IS ONE OF the planet's most prolific crops. In fact, this fluffy, white plant supplies over half of the world's fiber needs, from jeans and t-shirts to towels, food products, and tampons. In 2004, cotton's reach resulted in a $334 billion industry. This cash cow is grown in over 60 countries, including China, India, and Turkey, but the U.S. is the world's second-largest cotton producer.

Despite its pure, clean appearance, cotton is a crop that is grown utilizing an astounding amount of pesticides due to its vulnerability to attack by insects. Would you believe that up to $2.6 billion worth of pesticides are used worldwide on cotton each year?

Today, just 2.4 percent of the world's arable land is planted with cotton, but cotton farming employs 25 percent of all global insecticide use and over 10 percent of the world's pesticide use (including insecticides, herbicides, and defoliants). It is one of the most pesticide-intensive crops on the planet, ranking third in pesticide use after corn and soybeans.

Across the U.S., a whopping 55 million pounds of pesticides were used on the nearly 10 million acres of cotton planted in 2008. While the EPA and individual states regulate and monitor pesticide use, the World Health Organization has

Cotton crops are abundant in the U.S., as is hazardous pesticide use. ©istockphoto.com/David Sucsy

classified most of the pesticides commonly used on cotton as either "Highly Hazardous" or "Moderately Hazardous." Many of these pesticides, including the commonly used organophosphates and carbamates, are possible and known carcinogens as well as nervous system toxins.

These chemicals can affect our health in a variety of ways, including making their way into our water supply, into our air via pesticide "drift," and into the products we use. While feeding pesticide-ridden "gin trash" (cotton's leftover leaves, stems, and short fibers) to livestock has become illegal in California, this byproduct is still used to make mattresses, tampons, and cotton balls elsewhere.

What Is Genetically Engineered Cotton?

A SCIENTIFIC MARVEL of the modern growing age, genetically engineered (GE) cotton (along with GE corn and soybeans) was introduced in the 1990s by agricultural giants Calgene and Monsanto. GE plants are created by splicing foreign genetic material into plant genomes, a process that creates a new organism that is not present in the natural world. The cotton debuted by these companies was genetically engineered with its own built-in pest defenses derived from Bacillus Thuringiensis (Bt). The philosophy was that this crop could reduce the need for pesticide use and, in the end, yield more cotton.

Bt is a naturally occurring soil bacterium that would cause certain insects feeding upon it to cease feeding and perish within a few days. It had been used safely, albeit sparingly, by both conventional and organic farmers for decades. It was commonly thought that frequent use of Bt would lead to a resistance among useful insects and, thus, the loss of a crucial pest control tool.

As such, a growing number of scientists predict that constant exposure to the engineered Bt in GE cotton fields will lead to a widespread resistance by insects and the ultimate return to the use of chemical herbicides. There is also concern that the Bt gene can be transferred to the wild relatives of cotton, affecting the natural ecosystem. In addition, research has shown the Bt toxin, which is present in every cell of the engineered plant including its roots, may leach into soil and potentially harm soil microorganisms and cause a disruption to the soil ecology.

Monsanto has also brought Roundup Ready cotton to the market; this genetically engineered cotton plant holds the promise not to perish when cotton fields are sprayed with toxic weed killers such as glyphostate and bromoxynil. Despite these advances, even the world's genetically engineered cotton crop still requires tons of herbicides and insecticides for production each year.

GE cotton is also used to make cottonseed oil, which is present in many foods. ©istockphoto.com/Brasil2

The use of GE cotton has grown in leaps and bounds. In 2007, herbicide-tolerant (HT) cotton like Roundup Ready was planted on 70 percent of the U.S.'s cotton acreage. Bt cotton was utilized on 59 percent of all cotton farming acreage in 2007, as well. Around the world, only about 20 percent of cotton is GE. Because the overall effects on the planet's natural ecosystem remain relatively unknown, genetically engineered crops like Bt cotton and Roundup Ready cotton are a hotly debated topic.

Adding Organic Cotton Into Your Closet

THE GREEN SOLUTION TO the cotton conundrum is to buy products made with organic cotton, which delivers a soft and natural feel plus a green report card. Organic cotton is grown using methods that are easy on the earth. Its production focuses on maintaining soil fertility while reducing the use of toxic insecticides, herbicides, and fertilizers.

Due to consumers' interest in the earth-friendly benefits of organic cotton products, global production has increased by a whopping 53 percent from the 2005/2006 season to 2006/2007. According to the Organic Exchange, global organic cotton sales were projected to spike to $2.6 billion by the end of 2008 (up from $583 million in 2005). The U.S. currently produces only about 3 percent of the world's organic cotton.

The best way to get started is to look for organic cotton basics in everything from t-shirts and underwear to socks when you need to replace these items. Organic basics are more readily available today than ever before—you can find them at many mainstream chain stores (even Walmart sells organic cotton basics) and online retailers such as www.ecowise.com. The cost differential for these products, especially at discount retailers, is minimal for basic items. When factors like style and brand name enter the organic cotton arena, prices tend to inch up a bit higher.

Cost Meter: **$** to **$$**

Organic cotton products are now available at all price levels. ©istockphoto.com/Oktay Ortakcioglu

Look for the certified organic stamp on any products you buy—it shows that your cotton has been third-party certified to be organic. By putting your money into more earth-friendly, sustainable products, you will help fan the flame of increasing demand for organic and sustainable cotton products, which, in turn, will encourage more farmers to convert their farmland into pesticide-free zones.

Green Idea

Because organic cotton production is costly to farmers—and to manufacturers and retailers as a result—there is a movement afoot in the U.S. to help more farmers convert to farming practices that are more sustainable and use fewer pesticides, even if they are not certified organic. This direction has been launched by the Sustainable Cotton Project (SCP), which works directly with conventional growers to help them implement reduced-risk farming methods that work for them. The result of the SCP's efforts is a new product called Cleaner Cotton. The SCP says that, in 2007, two organic cotton farmers growing 240 acres in California reduced chemical use by just over 500 pounds. In contrast, the 22 farmers growing Cleaner Cotton on 2,000 acres reduced chemical use by about 2,000 pounds. You can also look for the sustainable Cleaner Cotton moniker in-store when shopping for greener clothing.

Clothing Production, Chemicals, and Your Health

ONCE A FIBER LIKE cotton has made its way through harvesting, it goes through a number of production processes before it lands as a finished garment on a rack in a store. These typically also involve potentially harmful chemicals, many of which are found as residues in the finished product. Do these affect our health?

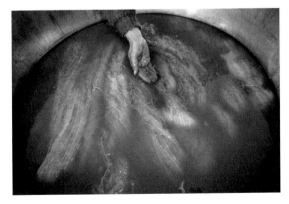

How do processing dyes and chemicals affect us?
©istockphoto.com/Daniel MAR

Some studies indicate the presence of these chemicals may, in fact, affect the health of the wearer, causing allergies, eczema, and even cancer. One example is the now-banned benzidine, a manufactured chemical that was used to produce dyes and has been linked to an increased risk of bladder cancer. In addition, most conventional fabric dyes contain carcinogenic heavy metals like arsenic and mercury as well as formaldehyde, a skin irritant that has also been linked to cancer.

Green Idea

After harvest, all cotton endures a litany of processes to reach its final stages. One of these is bleaching, where cotton is whitened with chlorine bleach. This process releases the carcinogen dioxin, which is a known hormone disruptor. Toxic dyes are also used in many cases to color cotton products. The best way to be green and avoid these unhealthy and polluting processes is to choose organic cotton products that are not bleached and dyed—or that are dyed with low-impact pigments.

A Danish study was completed in 2000 by the country's Environmental Protection Agency. The report, entitled "Chemicals in Textiles," found that chemicals in clothing could cause skin irritations, allergic reactions, asthma, and bronchitis. The study's researchers found 27 substances that they denoted as an environmental risk (from washing out of clothing into sewage systems) as well as a health risk to retail store workers and consumers. These included nicotine, phthalates, and heavy metals such as lead, tin, arsenic, and mercury.

There are few sure-fire ways to avoid all of the chemicals involved in a garment's production from start to finish. Unbleached organic cotton is an excellent start. Some clothing brands are touting their products as "Azo-Free," which means they are free of potentially carcinogenic azo dyes. Others promote their products as having "low-impact" dyes. To date, neither of these claims is monitored or regulated. In the end, when adding new pieces into your wardrobe, your best bet is to look for earth-conscious clothing brands that focus on the integrity of their garments' manufacture.

Eco Fact

Did you know the main ingredient in polyester is petroleum? To manufacture the prolific polyester fiber, crude oil is broken down into petrochemicals and converted with heat. In addition to depleting our fossil fuel supply, polyester production also releases nitrogen and carbon dioxide into the air.

Choosing Earth-Friendly Fabrics

I N ADDITION TO organic cotton, there are several other alternative fabrics coming into the eco spotlight today. Most are more sustainable because their production involves fewer pesticides for growing and less chemicals for processing. As you buy new pieces to complement your wardrobe in the future, consider purchasing clothing that has an eco conscience.

The Beauty of Bamboo

Because bamboo is the world's fastest-growing plant, it is also the world's most sustainable crop. This tall, lanky plant is actually classified as a grass and not a tree; it regenerates itself quickly thanks to a fast-spreading root network. Bamboo can also improve soil quality in the areas in which it grows.

Cost Meter: **$** to **$$**

Bamboo accounts for 35 percent of the fibers in the Bamboo Crew socks from Bridgedale. ©Bridgedale

In addition, bamboo boasts a built-in natural defense against bacteria, meaning that it does not require the use of pesticides to grow abundantly. This natural feature also translates itself into the bamboo fiber, even after it has been processed. This lends an anti-bacterial quality to clothing produced with bamboo fibers, which are also notably odor-resistant and hypoallergenic. One study conducted by the China Industrial Testing Center found that bacteria introduced to a bamboo fabric were reduced by 99.8 percent in a 24-hour period.

Some species of bamboo can grow up to four feet in one day. ©istockphoto.com/pixhook

123

As a fabric, bamboo delivers a soft, silky feel due to its smooth and round fiber structure. It is a good choice for active endeavors because it is highly absorbent and breathable; it also remains two degrees cooler against the skin than wool or cotton. Of note is that bamboo does have some downsides, including the fact that processing does require the use of caustic soda and other chemicals.

Hallowed Hemp

Hemp was the first plant that was cultivated for its fiber for use in making cloth and clothing. Its bast fibers, which come from the stalk of the plant, are one of the longest and softest natural fibers on the planet. Hemp fabric is also naturally mold and mildew resistant. Hemp is another incredibly fast-growing plant that requires little to no pesticides or herbicides to grow. It is, in fact, used to control weeds in areas where other crops are growing. Hemp also gives back to the earth by controlling erosion of topsoil and producing oxygen.

Hemp is the commonly accepted name for all plants in the genus Cannabis, but the "industrial hemp" used in the manufacture of everything from clothing and textiles to paper and foods is only distantly related to the Cannabis plant well-known for its use as a medicinal and recreational drug. Industrial hemp, which is produced primarily in Canada, France, and China, contains below .3 percent of THC, while Cannabis grown for marijuana can contain anywhere from 6 to 20 percent of this psychoactive drug.

Hemp requires little to no pesticides to grow.
©istockphoto.com/Richard Stamper

The upscale upstart Viridis Luxe uses hemp in a wide variety of its luxurious clothing designs. ©Andreea Radutoiu

In North America, the retail market for hemp textiles and fabrics is booming; it surpassed $100 million in 2007 and is expected to continue growing at a rate of 10 percent a year, according to the Hemp Industries Association. Until recently, the U.S. remained as the only "first world" country that was not planting industrial hemp, even though our country is one of the largest importers. In June of 2008, a state law was passed to allow farmers to begin planting industrial hemp in Vermont.

Today, hemp has become a darling of the fashion world and is used by both moderately priced clothing brands and a variety of notable couture designers in making style-driven clothing. It is often combined with luxury fabrics such as silk, linen, or cashmere and styled into soft, modern silhouettes. Additionally, brands such as Holden deliver hemp-based clothing for active endeavors and an entire website, www.hempest.com, has been devoted to the sales of clothing and other products made from industrial hemp.

The Power of Wool

The use of wool as a textile dates all the way back to 1500 B.C. It has a long and storied history as a fabric that provides incredible temperature control—giving warmth in cool weather (even when wet) and displaying outstanding cooling properties even when the heat rises. Sheared from sheep, wool is naturally resistant to bacteria, mold, and mildew; Merino is typically considered the gold standard. Wool is also a sustainable fiber that does not require the use of fossil fuels in its production.

Wool is a truly renewable resource. ©Icebreaker

There are also some downsides to wool. The presence of pests like ticks and lice in sheep's wool causes farmers to sometimes dip their animals in organophosphate pesticides, an act that creates health risks for the animals, the farm workers, and the local water supply. Other animals undergo mulesing, where strips of wool-bearing skin are removed to control parasites. Some herds of sheep are also regularly given hormones and antibiotics to increase their yields.

To ensure your wool is earth- and animal-friendly, look for clothing manufacturers that provide a "transparent" supply chain (meaning they reveal how they produce and process their products) or those that use certified organic or Pure Grow Wool. The latter is a program that designates that its farmers use no chemicals, pesticides, or artificial materials in their sheep's environment. In addition, all grazing pastures must be free of pesticides for at least two years and any supplemental feed is organic. Shearing takes place in a clean and humane manner. Finally, the packing and cleaning process for the shorn wool must be chemical-free as well.

While Pure Grow and organic wool products can be slightly more expensive, these products are durable, meaning you will get your money's worth and your eco-conscience will rest easy. In the past few years, wool apparel has been gaining in popularity, especially in active and sport applications. Part of this is due to modern design philosophies that present wool clothing that is soft, comfortable, stylish, and efficient.

Green Idea

Soy fabric, made from proteins extracted during the making of tofu, was developed in China in the late 1990s and is also gaining popularity as a more earth-friendly choice for clothing, especially since it minimizes waste and does not require any additional pesticides or herbicides for its production.

The Icebreaker Merino wool clothing company utilizes sustainable production, ethical manufacturing, and a transparent supply chain. ©Icebreaker

Choosing Recycled Clothing

AN INSPIRING RESPONSE to the world's mounting problems with the disposal of plastic PET bottles (like those used for soda, water, etc.) is the development of recycled fibers like Eco-fi (formerly known as Ecospun). Eco-fi is a high-quality polyester fiber made from 100-percent-certified recycled plastic PET bottles—it is used for textile products ranging from jackets and pants to home furnishings and carpets.

This modern, eco-conscious fiber has inherent properties such as strength, softness, and shrinkage-resistance and it is often blended with other fibers like cotton and wool. It takes about ten plastic PET bottles to make one pound of Eco-fi fiber. It is estimated that Eco-fi has the capacity to keep almost three billion plastic bottles out of landfills each year and eliminate 400,000 tons of planet-affecting emissions.

Cost Meter:

COOLMAX has also recently launched a similar fiber called EcoTech, which has a performance focus. It is also made from recycled plastic bottles.

It just doesn't get much more sustainable than taking a product out of the waste stream and using it to replace other products that utilize fossil fuels in their manufacture. Clothing containing recycled fibers is becoming much more readily available and prices remain on par or just slightly higher than conventional pieces.

Patagonia delivers an eco-friendly package in this top, which is made from 37 percent recycled polyester and 63 percent chlorine-free Merino wool. ©Patagonia

About 10 plastic bottles go into the making of Billabong's Project BLUE Shockwave boardshort, which is made from Eco-Supreme recycled PET material. ©Billabong

The Green Style Movement

AN ECO-FRIENDLY COLLECTIVE design consciousness has emerged in the fashion world, meaning that those who are fashion-conscious *and* eco-conscious no longer have to sacrifice style. A variety of designers are getting into the game, from Donna Karan, who runs the Urban Zen initiative which markets organic and natural fashions, to Stella McCartney, who has always put the onus on environmentally sound style.

Cost Meter: **$**

This direction also means that the environment is taking center stage, right on the runways of the world. In fact, in 2008, hemp hit the height of style when clothing made of the sustainable fiber by well-known designers was on display in the FutureFashion eco-fashion show that was housed at the Barneys New York flagship store. To give it extra punch, this event coincided with New York Fashion Week, where all the major American designers present their new collections on the runway.

High style takes the high road; lines like Viridis Luxe focus on using sustainable fabrics and production methods. ©Andreea Radutoiu

Even purveyors of fashion are getting into the eco game. In 2007, Saks Fifth Avenue converted its extravagant Fifth Avenue Christmas display to LED lights, which drastically reduced energy consumption. The luxury department store chain also has an online shop, called "Green House: Home of Eco Smart Style," for eco-conscious designer fashions and jewelry made from recycled materials.

Such a movement was sure to spawn an eco-fashion magazine. Today, the newly launched Boho Magazine (www.bohomag.com) is solely focused on eco-conscious, stylish living.

Eco-conscious consumers have so many choices today that it's easy to add green pieces into their wardrobe. It is important, however, to be on the lookout for "greenwashing," which is defined by those manufacturers and retailers who simply capitalize on the earth-friendly trend by touting their merchandise as green even if it is not.

Some companies are combating this by offering product traceability, a feature that reveals a supply chain that is truly eco-friendly. For example, Walmart offers an inside look into its Love, Earth jewelry line by unveiling where it is sourced and produced. New Zealand-based Icebreaker even offers a "Baacode" on its wool products; consumers who enter this specific number into Icebreaker's website can learn about the farm where their wool was produced and learn about the manufacturing process. By choosing to support ethical clothing companies and putting your money into the green fashion movement, you will make a significant impact on its future growth.

Green on the Cheap

Green style doesn't have to be expensive. After successfully rolling out clothing lines made with hemp, bamboo, organic cotton, and soy apparel in Canada, the discount mega-retailer COSTCO has recently introduced an organic cotton clothing program with HTnaturals in the United States.

Buying Green Accessories

AS WITH CLOTHING, there can be a wealth of problems involved with the production of everything from shoes to handbags. Many accessories are fashioned with leather that, at first glance, may appear to be a renewable, earth-friendly resource. But, leather is tanned using a toxic mixture of chemicals, including mineral salts, formaldehyde, and oils and dyes that are oftentimes cyanide-based. These chemicals are concerning because they can harm workers and get flushed into the water supply if not properly disposed of.

Another un-green option for the manufacture of accessories is polyvinyl chloride, which is better known as vinyl or PVC. During production, PVC gives off dioxins that are considered to be harmful carcinogens that may attack the immune system. Additionally, PVC also contains chemicals called phthalates, which are believed to cause reproductive disorders. Like vinyl shower curtains, PVC accessories can also off-gas these chemicals into the air in your home (and elsewhere) when they are new.

There are earth-friendly options for accessories today, including products made from sustainable fibers like organic cotton, hemp, soy, or wool. Some makers of leather accessories also offer products that have more integrity than those which are conventionally produced. When shopping for accessories to fill a functional need or simply update your wardrobe, be on the lookout for items that are clearly green in one way or another.

Cost Meter: **$**

Green on the Cheap

Payless ShoeSource has launched a line of affordable, earth-friendly shoes and handbags made from materials like hemp, organic cotton, and linen. The shoes, which will be produced using biodegradable glues and recycled rubber outsoles, will ship in recycled boxes and retail for an average of under $30.

The new END Footwear line focuses on creating shoes that have the least amount of impact on the earth as possible. ©END Footwear

Green Review:
Changes to Focus on During Week Five

1. Look for organic cotton options when shopping for basic clothing items like t-shirts, socks, underwear, and pajamas.

2. When shopping for other clothing items like pants, shirts, and activewear, look for eco-friendly materials like hemp, bamboo, soy, and sustainably produced wool.

3. Also look for clothing companies that offer "transparency," which is a view into their manufacturing methods and environmental impacts.

4. To help keep untold amounts of plastic bottles out of landfills, choose products made with the recycled PET fibers Eco-fi or EcoTech when you are shopping for new wardrobe items.

5. Recycle your own unwanted clothing (instead of sending it to a landfill) by taking it a Salvation Army or Goodwill location.

6. When feasible, choose eco-conscious accessories that are made from recycled or earth-friendly materials.

©istockphoto.com/Floortje

TrueGreen: Choosing a Green Dry Cleaner

WHEN IT COMES TO CARING for our best suits, dresses, and sweaters, most of us head straight to the dry cleaner for gentle, consistent care in a professional environment. But, what many consumers don't know is that the majority of cleaners across America use an incredibly toxic chemical to process their clothes—one that could also be harming their health.

Perchloroethylene (also know as perc or tetra-chloroethylene) is widely used for dry-cleaning fabrics but it is a harmful solvent that the EPA declares is of known human toxicity and also a hazardous air pollutant. Its short-term health effects include headaches, nausea, and dizziness; it is also believed to cause infertility and some cancers in cases of long-term exposure. In fact, a Consumers Union study has reported that consumers who wear newly dry-cleaned clothing once a week over a 40-year span could breathe in enough perc to increase their risk of cancer by 150 times.

A 2006 ruling on air toxics standards includes a phase-out of perc machines located in residential buildings by 2020.
©istockphoto.com/ Frances Twitty

About 85 percent of the estimated 25,000 to 35,000 dry cleaners across the country still use about 140 gallons of perc each year. This chemical can easily make its way into the air supply (it is a contributor to smog) and groundwater, thus potentially contaminating local drinking water. Up until the mid-1980s, it was legal for dry cleaners to pour perc right down the drain.

A few alternative dry-cleaning options are emerging, but these are not available in every area. Wet cleaning is a much greener process that utilizes water and biodegradable soaps, but quality results can be spotty, so try to get a recommendation for a cleaner using this method. Another eco-conscious process uses liquid carbon dioxide, but the detergents used contain potentially harmful volatile organic compounds. You can locate a greener cleaner near you by checking out www.nodryclean.com or you can limit your exposure to perc by following this short tip list from the Sierra Club:

1. Remove the wrapper from your dry-cleaned clothing outside or in the garage instead of inside your home and let clothing air out for four to five days before wearing.

2. As you update your wardrobe, look to clothing that does not require dry cleaning.

3. Dry clean clothing only when absolutely necessary—experts recommend spot cleaning regularly and dry cleaning once a year.

4. Confirm that your dry cleaner has a certified waste hauler to remove perc, which helps ensure it does not make its way into your local drinking water and ecosystems.

SuperGreen:
Buying Fine Jewelry with a Conscience

WHETHER YOU'RE READY to take the plunge into matrimonial bliss and buy that wedding ring or are coveting a glamorous new piece of luxury jewelry, a little bit of awareness will help you do it in a manner that is respectful of the earth and its inhabitants. The mining of metals like gold and silver and the trade of gemstones like diamonds can be hazardous to both.

The use and disposal of cyanide, a well-known poison, comes into play with gold mining. Cyanide solutions are used to dissolve and extract gold, but they are acutely toxic to humans and even more harmful to wildlife, which can react severely even to low exposures. These solutions can also leach into groundwater and soil, causing additional environmental concerns. A breach in a tailings dam at a gold mine in Romania in 2000 released 100,000 cubic meters of cyanide-ridden waste. The results were devastating—nearly all the fish in local waters were killed and drinking water was shut off for over 2.5 million people.

Buying a "conflict diamond" supports brutal war efforts in impoverished African countries.
©istockphoto.com/Mark Evans

What can you do to support sustainable mining practices and minimize your jewelry's impact on the planet? Beyond purchasing antique or estate jewelry to extend its useful life or recycling old gold into new forms, consumers can ask their jeweler where—and how—their gold or silver was mined. Other resources for responsible mining are www.responsiblegold.org and www.greenkarat.com.

When it comes to diamonds, you may already be familiar with the well-publicized social issues involved with diamond trading. Sometimes called "blood diamonds" or "conflict diamonds," these precious, sparkling gemstones are the subject of great controversy. Almost half of the world's diamonds are mined in war-racked African nations, where they are sold to finance war efforts or a warlord's activities.

When purchasing a diamond for any purpose, check with your jewelry retailer to ensure that it is a conflict-free diamond, from which the profits were not used to fund wars or mined under unethical conditions. You can also ask for a KPCS (Kimberly Process Certification Scheme) Certificate of Origin. This program was implemented by a large group of diamond-trading countries in 2002 to set standards to stop illegally traded conflict diamonds from entering the ethical diamond market. Remember that only certified diamonds can be traced to their source. This choice may cost you a little bit more for the final purchase but your clear conscience will last a lifetime.

Living naturally without harmful chemicals is a beautiful thing.
©istockphoto.com/Quavondo Nguyen

Week Six: Green Is Beautiful

THE TYPICAL AMERICAN ROUTINE involves waking up and preparing to head into the world—but not before applying a litany of personal care products. We shower with soap, shampoo, and conditioner and lather up with shaving cream. We clean our teeth with a dollop of toothpaste and rub on some deodorant. Many slather on moisturizers, put on makeup, and swish around some mouthwash. The grand finale often includes splashing on a touch of aftershave or perfume.

The personal care products industry rings in about $40 billion a year. It's no wonder—a survey of over 2,300 people conducted by the Environmental Working Group (EWG) determined that the average adult uses nine personal care products each day (one quarter of women surveyed, however, used at least 15 products). The caveat of the study was that EWG determined these nine products were concocted with an array of 126 unique chemical ingredients.

While the personal care process makes us feel particularly polished and clean, it is typically anything but green. As a matter of fact, many of the ingredients in average, everyday personal care products are hazardous chemicals that can make their way into our bloodstreams and cells plus the water supply of our neighborhoods and local ecosystems.

This chapter will share the downsides of beauty and personal care products and define how you can find safer, chemical-free selections. Because when it comes to the health of the planet and your family, green is particularly beautiful.

Beauty Is More Than Skin Deep

THE PREPONDERANCE OF personal care products—from simple soap and toothpaste to specialized creams and a palette of makeup—on the market today help make us feel that we need an arsenal to keep ourselves clean and polished. This belief is bolstered by the force of the multi-million-dollar ad campaigns that accompany these products.

Unfortunately, this could be bad for our health, in large part, because the personal care product industry remains relatively unregulated. The U.S. Food and Drug Administration (FDA) places no restrictions on the ingredients that go into making beauty products—it actually looks to the makers of these products to conduct their own safety testing but does not require them to do so.

According to the EWG, nearly 90 percent of the 10,500 ingredients that the FDA has determined are used in personal care products have never been tested for safety by any group or organization, including the FDA and the industry's self-policing safety panel. As a result, most conventional products are packed with ingredients of a dubious nature, including known human carcinogens, endocrine disruptors, and toxins like coal tar. Some even contain harmful components like lead, mercury, and petroleum byproducts.

We put this mix right onto our skin and into our mouths, which is how they get direct access to our body's systems. Our skin is the largest organ in our bodies—and it absorbs everything we put onto it. Unlike food, which is filtered by our stomachs, what we put on our skin can head directly into our bloodstream. In fact, studies have discovered common cosmetic ingredients in human tissue, including preservative parabens in breast tumor tissue.

The inhabitants of your bathroom cabinet may have a dark side. ©istockphoto.com/Kevin Brown

The affects of personal care products don't stop with human health; they extend directly into the environment. A Centers for Disease Control and Prevention study on human exposure to plasticizers called phthalates found that this common personal care product ingredient ended up in the urine samples of study subjects. Via human excretions, along with being washed down the drain in the shower and tub, these chemicals are entering the water supply chain and possibly passing through treatment plants and out to affect wildlife. Some studies have also found the presence of personal care product ingredients in rivers and streams in the U.S.

If you're wondering how all of this has happened, you are not alone. A number of large consumer-interest groups have been calling for reform to this dysfunctional system for years. What can you do to protect yourself and the planet?

Do Some Housecleaning in the Bathroom

THE FIRST STEP IN CLEANSING yourself of the chemical cocktails in your toiletries is to rid your bathroom of its most harmful inhabitants. Grab your shampoos, toothpastes, hand soaps, body washes, creams and lotions, and cosmetics and place them all on a well-lit countertop where you can line up the defendants. Use the list on the next two pages to compare and contrast the ingredients in each. You may need a small magnifying glass to take a hard look at the ingredients found in the label's fine print.

Do they contain any—or perhaps several—of the most offensive ingredients? If so, you may just want to toss this product in the trash and save your body the burden of dealing with the harmful chemicals you're using every day.

Cost Meter: **$** to **$$**

Which items need to go? ©istockphoto.com/Steve Smith

If the ingredient roundup doesn't appear harmful at first glance but the list appears long and unfamiliar, you may simply want to use up the product and then convert to a natural alternative. No doubt, it would be an expensive endeavor to replace all the products in your bathroom at once. So, rid yourself of the worst and replace the others with healthier, more planet-friendly options as they run out.

And remember, just because a manufacturer touts its product as "organic" or "all-natural" doesn't mean that it is. Be wary of any claims like this, especially if the ingredient list doesn't contain "certified organic" ingredients or it looks like a chemical concoction.

You may also want to determine if you can use fewer products in the future and decrease your risk and impact. Another positive, wide-sweeping move is to choose fragrance-free products. Fragrances are usually harsh chemicals that can cause allergic reactions, so scan your product's ingredient label—if the word "fragrance" appears there, it is not fragrance-free.

10 Key Ingredients to Avoid

The following is a list of the 10 most offensive ingredients to watch out for, some of which have been culled from the EWG's "What Not to Buy" List. If you can keep these ingredients out of the products you use, you're off to a good start.

1. **Triclosan:** This ingredient, which is used in nearly all antibacterial products from soaps to toothpastes, has been detected in studies of nursing mother's breast milk. It produces carcinogenic and birth-defect-causing dioxins when exposed to sunlight, which means it also harms the environment. There is also concern that antibacterial products, which wipe out all bad *and* good bacteria, will cause bacteria resistance in the future.

2. **Phthalates:** This chemical is a plasticizer that has been shown to cause male sex organ damage such as sperm damage and infertility. Its presence in nail polish is also a concern, especially for pregnant women. Watch out for it in your products; it usually hides under the moniker "Fragrance."

Green on the Cheap

The EWG offers an excellent source for information on a vast array of products on the market today via its Skin Deep cosmetic safety database, www.cosmeticsdatabase.com. It actually pairs ingredients in over 38,000 products against 50 toxicity and regulatory databases and provides toxicity ratings for each product and ingredient. The site allows you to enter a product category or even a specific product's name to gain further information about ingredients and their danger level.

3. **Fragrance:** Fragrances, in general, are good to avoid because they are a "loophole" ingredient—companies don't have to reveal any of the potentially hundreds of chemicals in fragrances. As such, they often hide endocrine-disrupting phthalates, among other things. While a good-smelling product can be appealing, know that its ultimate consequences may not be.

4. **Parabens:** This preservative is highly common in toiletries but it can break down into a form that causes estrogenic activity in human breast cancer cells. It can show up on labels in many forms, including butyl-, ethyl-, isobutyl-, methyl-, and propylparaben.

5. **Petroleum Byproducts:** It may be hard to believe, but petroleum is a hardworking, prolific ingredient in the cosmetics industry—it shows up in everything from face cream to baby shampoo. Steer clear of any product that lists any form of petroleum or liquid paraffin (also known as mineral oil) as an ingredient.

6. **Hydroquinone:** Even the FDA has recently warned against using skin lighteners with this allergenic ingredient, which is a potential carcinogen. This bleaching chemical can also cause ochronosis, a skin disease that causes lesions.

7. **Coal Tar:** This known carcinogen is utilized as an active ingredient in dandruff shampoos, anti-itch creams, and product dyes like FD&C Blue 1, which is used in toothpaste, and FD&C Green 3, which is used in mouthwash.

8. **Nanoparticles:** These trendy, tiny particles are touted as making products like sunscreen more blendable, but some experts believe they may also damage brain cells and red blood cells. Nanoparticles are extremely difficult to ID on ingredient labels—either look for "nano metals" or "buckeyeballs" or buy products that claim to not have this ingredient in their mix.

9. **1,4-Dioxane:** Also called dioxane, this ingredient, which is a known animal carcinogen and a probable human carcinogen, is frequently used as a solvent in items like shampoo and body wash. Look for it in products marked as containing sodium laureth sulfate and also those that contain "PEG," "polyethylene," "polyethylene glycol," "polyoxyethylene," "polyethoxyethylene," or "polyoxynolethylene."

10. **Mercury and Lead:** Brain-damaging mercury can show up as thimerosal or phenyl mercuric acetate in some mascara brands. Lead, which has been banned by the government from house paint, is still common as lead acetate in black hair dyes for men and in hydrated silica, a toothpaste ingredient.

Reading Ingredient Labels Before You Buy

YOUR BEST DEFENSE is a good offense with personal care products—today, reading ingredient labels before you buy is a crucial step to self-preservation. You'll also be doing your part to make sure the chemicals in these products don't impact the planet.

As such, your next step is to become a label-conscious, informed consumer and buy only products that feature ingredients you can live with. In fact, besides buying truly organic and natural products, the best thing you can do is to take the time to stop in the store aisle and carefully read the label of what you're contemplating to buy before you do so.

Eco Fact

The concern about cosmetics and other personal care products extends far beyond the health concerns involved with their daily use. Since these products often contain a variety of industrial chemicals, they also need to be kept out of the reach of children. According to the American Association of Poison Control Centers, more than one million poisonings of children under the age of six were reported in 2002 from the ingestion of household products, with cosmetics and personal care products at the top of the "poisons" list.

Cost Meter: $0

Know before you swish. ©istockphoto.com/Claudio Baldini

Use the list provided on the previous page to take the chemicals and toxins out of your daily repertoire. You can photocopy it and take it along on your next shopping excursion. Soon enough, you'll have these harmful ingredients memorized and be able to breeze through the aisles, picking the products that are toxin-free. Your due diligence will be a savvy move that will help preserve your health and the health of the environment as well. For, as you can see, conventional beauty and personal care products' reach is definitely more than skin deep.

Switching to "Green" Personal Care Products

IN ADDITION TO scanning ingredient labels before you buy, looking for truly natural and certified organic personal care products will take your toiletries back to basics. Many of these greener options are equally as (or even more) effective as their conventional counterparts. Due to consumer awareness of the health risks with conventional products, the natural personal care market is growing in leaps and bounds. In fact, according to a report published by Packaged Facts, the market surpassed $2.6 billion in 2004, a number that represented over 50 percent growth since 1998. Most natural personal care products are only slightly higher in price, a fact that will keep your budget intact when shopping for the items that will stock your bathroom cabinets.

Green up your bathroom with chemical-free products.
©istockphoto.com/Pali Rao

Cost Meter:

Where can you shop for natural products? Your local health food store will likely have a solid selection of products you can count on, but you can always fall back on your label-reading skills just to be sure. Many other conventional stores, including chain grocery and drug stores, do offer an alternative selection of products that are mostly chemical-free, as well. Additionally, there is a wealth of online retailers and companies that focus on the pure and natural:

- ▶ **www.futurenatural.com**
- ▶ **www.apeacefulcompany.com**
- ▶ **www.bewellstaywell.com**
- ▶ **www.drhauschka.com**
- ▶ **www.sheaterraorganics.com**
- ▶ **www.sukipure.com**
- ▶ **www.moporganics.com**
- ▶ **www.live-live.com**
- ▶ **www.tomsofmaine.com**
- ▶ **For a listing of even more companies that make natural personal care products, check out www.greenproductsalliance.com.**

There are so many products to consider, you may be left wondering where to begin even after you've purged your cabinets of the worst offenders. Read on for specific information on and warnings about some of the key items you likely use every day and how to protect the planet and your health with natural choices. If knowledge is power, then this primer will hopefully help empower and give you the ability to make positive, eco-friendly changes in your day-to-day life.

Lathering Up

Soaps, facial cleansers, bubble bath, shower gels, and shampoos lather up with fluffy, thick bubbles that make us feel impeccably clean. Interestingly, it is the creation of this feature that can make these products anything but healthy. Most of the conventional versions of these products are made with surfactants, a chemical that enhances a product's bubbling and spreading abilities.

Surfactants fall under a group of chemicals called sulfates, typically listed as sodium lauryl sulfate (SLS) and sodium laureth sulfate (SLES) on product labels, and the related chemicals diethanolamine (DEA), monoethanolomine (MEA), and triethanolomine (TEA). Watch out for these ingredient list busters as well; they can severely dry out skin and hair, contain petroleum, and, even worse, create the carcinogen dioxane as a byproduct.

Are your bubbles derived from sulfates?
©istockphoto.com/Jyn Meyer

Read your labels and look for products that promote themselves as "sulfate-free." You might get a lower sudsing action in these cleansers, but you'll rest easy knowing you're putting fewer toxins into your system—and down the drain into the water supply.

Another unusual ingredient that is common in shampoos, including baby shampoo, is formaldehyde, which is used in some preservatives. This potent chemical is a neurotoxin and a known cause for cancer, so be on the lookout for its presence in your products as well.

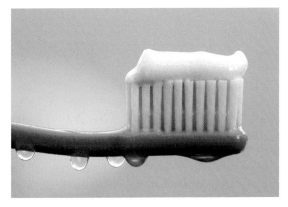

What's on your toothbrush?
©istockphoto.com/Duncan Walker

Green on the Cheap

Liquid and bar soaps are a multi-billion-dollar industry. When it comes to the bar, however, conventional and glycerin soaps are good options to avoid, because they typically contain phthalate-packed fragrances and harmful dyes. There are many inexpensive, natural bar soaps on the market today that use simple, effective ingredients.

Brushing Up

Plentiful suds have also become a part of our daily dental routine, which is due to the presence of sodium lauryl and laureth sulfates in toothpaste. The average tooth cleaning mixture is also packed with potentially carcinogenic parabens, sweeteners, and other chemicals in the form of artificial colors and flavors.

An EWG study, which tested 192 types of toothpaste, found some concerning results about the nature of a number of ingredients. A full 65 of the products contained potentially cancer-causing ingredients. Additionally, 44 percent contained harmful impurities and 19 percent were concocted with "penetration enhancers," which actually increase the user's exposure to the carcinogens and other potentially harmful ingredients contained in the product.

While there are numerous healthier options on the market today, picking out toothpaste that eliminates these harmful ingredients from its blend but also satisfies our dental care needs is tricky business. Some purely natural products may not give you the cavity protection you're looking for. If you're in the market for a product that will help ward off extra trips to the dentist, look for natural toothpaste that also offers a dose of fluoride.

Beyond health concerns, using toothpaste that contains dangerous chemicals can also affect our water supply. A 2007 study conducted of water samples taken from the San Francisco Bay found an amazing brew of potential toxins.

Researchers found phthalates, bisphenol A (BPA), and triclosan, all chemicals that are suspected of disrupting hormone systems in humans and wildlife. It is believed that these ingredients leached out of personal care products such as toothpaste and soap through household water systems. This research suggests that modern sewage treatment plants are not designed to capture the synthetic chemicals that are used in these types of products.

Eco Fact

All cosmetics and personal care product companies are required by law to post a warning label on products that have not been assessed for safety. The label should state: "Warning: The safety of this product has not been determined." While you might find this label on some products, it may be a moot point, as the industry's compliance with this is inconsistent. The FDA issued a warning to the industry in 2005, as a result of a petition from the EWG, stating that the agency was serious about enforcing the law. It is estimated that this kind of enforcement could result in the label appearing on more than 99 percent of the market's personal care products, not all of which have been tested for safety.

Sweat Equity

The first commercial deodorant was developed in 1888, but it wasn't until after World War II that Americans truly embraced the value of this odor-reducing product. Today, staying sweat- and odor-free in the U.S. has spawned a $2 billion industry of antiperspirants and deodorants in every incarnation imaginable, from solids to wipes.

What's the difference between a deodorant and an antiperspirant? While both work to combat odor, deodorants actually fight to inhibit the growth of the bacteria that cause odor. Antiperspirants, on the other hand, actually stop perspiration by blocking up the pores. Some believe this process actually keeps toxins in the body that would normally be purged through sweating.

Because of their different modes of operation, these two products fall under separate FDA classifications. Deodorants are listed as a cosmetic that functions only on the skin's surface. Antiperspirants rank as an over-the-counter drug because they change the way the body functions.

Stick deodorants can be packed with harmful ingredients. ©istockphoto.com/Lev Olkha

Both products do have one thing in common, which is a makeup that contains a number of chemicals that can be harmful to consumers. Deodorants contain the active ingredient triclosan, which is a widely used antibacterial agent. While triclosan is not necessarily immediately harmful to users, it is suspected that this ingredient could encourage bacterial resistance in the environment. In fact, a study by Tufts University Medical School in Boston found that triclosan's widespread use may be triggering bacteria to evolve strains that are resistant to antibacterial chemicals. This event would put people with weaker immune systems, such as children and the elderly, at greater risk to infection.

Deodorants also contain a mother lode (up to 80 percent of the entire product) of propylene glycol, a solvent that preserves moisture. It is also a potential neurotoxin that can trigger contact dermatitis, enlarged sweat glands, cysts, and respiratory irritation.

Antiperspirants cover both the odor and sweat front, but they also lay claim to some concerning ingredients. Number one is aluminum salts like aluminum chlorohydrate, the active ingredient in this product. These can also cause skin irritation and the cumulative effects of aluminum exposure have been linked to Alzheimer's disease.

About 20 years ago, scientists discovered that the brains of people with Alzheimer's displayed high levels of aluminum. At the time, many put the onus on aluminum-containing antiperspirants and eliminated those from their medicine cabinets. Since then, a variety of studies have batted the aluminum-Alzheimer's link back and forth with varying results.

The natural personal care market offers a wide variety of options that are less reliant on chemicals to get the job done. One solid choice is the unusual "crystal" or "rock" antiperspirant, which is composed of ammonium alum or potassium alum.

While chemical-derived fragrances are often used in conventional products, natural versions typically rely on bacteria-fighting herbs like rosemary, chamomile, and extracts of green tea. Look for these in the products you buy if a fresh scent is on your list of requirements. Also, because even natural stick deodorants contain propylene glycol, choose creams or roll-ons instead if you'd like to avoid this ingredient.

Protecting Safely

There is no denying the vitamin D-packed value and pure enjoyment of basking in the sun. But with the rewards of this infinitely renewable resource also comes risk. Skin cancer is the most common form of cancer in the U.S.—over one million cases are diagnosed each year. In fact, according to the Skin Cancer Foundation, one in five Americans will develop skin cancer over the course of their lifetime.

A daily dose of vitamin D can lower your cancer risk.
©istockphoto.com/Christian Wheatley

While these facts may make us want to slather on an extra helping of sunscreen before heading into the great outdoors, it's important to understand the downsides of sun protection, as well. A recent study conducted by the EWG looked at the ingredients of approximately 1,000 brand-name sunscreens. The findings included the fact that four out of five sunscreens evaluated either contained harmful chemicals or did not provide adequate protection from the sun's damaging rays.

Part of the problem lies in the fact that the FDA has yet to finalize the sunscreen standards that were announced over 30 years ago. Like all other personal care products, sunscreens remain relatively unregulated.

One of the more potent chemical ingredients in sunscreens is benzophene, which can cause rashes and has been shown to stimulate growth in breast cancer cells in some studies. Padimate-O, a derivative of PABA, is another potentially dangerous ingredient; in some studies it has caused DNA damage, which could be a precursor to cancer.

As you might imagine, there are also more natural sunscreen options available today, many of which can be found at your health food store. The EWG also offers a database of safer sunscreen options at http://cosmeticsdatabase.com/special/sunscreens2008/index.php.

Due to the nature of the product, some natural versions may still contain a few questionable ingredients, so sun worshipers may want to simply consider spending less time in the most harmful rays. Find some shade, stay indoors, or cover up properly during the hours between 10am and 4pm. Self-tanning creams also offer an excellent sun-free option to obtaining a bronzed tone; these have even been shown to reduce the risk of skin cancer because the chemically induced pigmentation absorbs a small amount of UV rays.

Green Idea

Is a daily dose of sun-drenched vitamin D important? A 2008 study published in the *Archives of Internal Medicine* showed that study participants with the lowest vitamin D levels had more than double the risk of dying from heart disease and other causes over an eight-year period compared with those with the highest levels of vitamin D. This valuable vitamin, which is produced naturally when the sun's ultraviolet rays hit the skin, has also been shown to decrease the risk of developing osteoporosis and various cancers. How much sun do you need to get your daily dose? Some estimates suggest that fair-skinned people should spend about 10 midday minutes outside daily and dark-skinned and elderly people could benefit from a few extra minutes. While the government recommends anywhere from 200 to 600 IUs daily, depending on age, many experts recommend up to 2,000 IUs, especially in the winter, when sunlight is in short supply.

Moisturizing Naturally

The beauty of moisturizers and lotions is that they help combat dry skin and the inevitable signs of aging. Today, there is every kind of body lotion and face moisturizer imaginable on the market—from eye creams and foot balms to anti-aging potions and simple body lotions. Moisturizers act as workhorses that combat dryness; they are fueled by such ingredients as water, plant-based or synthetic oils, humectants (which draw in moisture from the air), and occlusives, which seal the skin to stop moisture from escaping.

Does your lotion contain a chemical potion?
©istockphoto.com/Ryerson Clark

Some of these ingredients do have health and environmental effects. This is particularly concerning because moisturizers and lotions are leave-on products that do not get washed off like soaps, shampoos, and even sunscreen. As such, their cumulative effects can be much more significant.

The most-criticized offenders are the sealing occlusives, which are made with components like silicone and petrolatum (commonly known as petroleum jelly). These ingredients are both derived from non-renewable crude oil and their production depletes resources and inflicts pollution on the planet.

Moisturizers and lotions also typically contain paraben preservatives, which may be linked to the development of breast cancer. Some utilize coal tar colors. They also can boast a potpourri of synthetic fragrances, which can cause dizziness, headaches, rashes, and nausea.

Eco Fact

Another ingredient sometimes found in personal care products is placenta, and it is definitely a good one to avoid. According to the EWG, recent case studies have indicated that the hormones present in extracts from human and cow placenta, which is often used in beauty products because of its conditioning properties, may be enough to trigger breast growth in toddlers.

There has never been a better time to shop for more health- and earth-friendly moisturizers, as the options are plentiful. Head to the health food store or check out one of the online retailers listed later in this chapter. Look for simple, plant-based ingredients like aloe and oils such as olive, sunflower, apricot, and almond. Shea butter is also an excellent choice for moisturizing the body.

Accentuating Beautifully

Makeup is big business around the world and an important part of many cultures that place a high value on appearance. But, like most other personal care products, makeup is host to an incredible lineup of potentially harmful chemicals.

Many items, including foundations and powders, are home to parabens and other preservatives that are based in formaldehyde. Some contain synthetic fragrances and coloring agents that can be neurotoxic or carcinogenic. Even mascara has been found to contain mercury.

Nail polish is one of the worst perpetrators in the chemical game with its preponderance of phthalates, which can disrupt hormones; it is also a probable carcinogen and has been linked to birth defects. While there are a few natural options, it is highly recommended that women who are (or are considering to become) pregnant toss the nail polish for the time being and steer clear of nail salons where the air can be laced with a variety of harmful chemicals.

Many cosmetics contain phthalates, which have been linked to birth defects. ©istockphoto.com/PLAINVIEW

Additionally, a number of lipsticks and lipglosses contain petroleum jelly, which can be irritating and is derived from crude oil, as well as lead, which is a proven neurotoxin that is also linked to infertility and miscarriage. Product tests conducted by the Campaign for Safe Cosmetics in 2008 found lead in 61 percent of lipsticks tested with levels ranging up to .65 parts per million. Still, a bill was defeated in the Assembly Health Committee (even after passing in the California Senate) in 2008 to require lipstick manufacturers to produce their products with the least amount of lead.

While the continuing unregulated nature of cosmetics ingredients is disturbing, there is a light on the horizon. The Campaign for Safe Cosmetics, a coalition of women's, public health, labor, environmental health, and consumer rights groups, launched a campaign in 2002 to urge personal care products companies to sign a pledge to remove toxic chemicals from cosmetics and replace them with safer alternatives. This pledge, called the Compact for Safe Cosmetics, was developed after the release of the report "Not Too Pretty: Phthalates, Beauty Products, and the FDA," which found phthalates in nearly three quarters of all beauty products tested. To date, 600 companies have signed the Compact.

When you're shopping for cosmetics, look for those from the companies that have signed onto this pledge. You can view them at www.safecosmetics.org. There are also a growing number of natural cosmetic brands that use plant-based, chemical-free blends. Again, these products are just slightly higher in price than most conventional cosmetics. Look for them in your health food store or at a naturally focused online retailer.

Green Review:
Changes to Focus on During Week Six

1. Do some housecleaning in your bathroom cabinets and ditch the conventional personal care products that contain some of the most harmful chemicals, as noted in this chapter's list of "10 Key Ingredients to Avoid."

2. Photocopy the "10 Key Ingredients to Avoid" and take it along for any shopping excursions where you might be buying related products.

3. When shopping for a new personal care item, take the time to stop and read the label before you buy. Compare the ingredient list with the "10 Key Ingredients to Avoid" and focus on using products that don't contain these harmful chemicals.

4. As you run out of various cosmetics and personal care products, consider switching to more natural versions, which will limit your exposure to harmful chemicals. Look for these options for the products you use the most:

   ▶ **Soaps, Shampoos, and Cleansers**

   ▶ **Toothpaste**

   ▶ **Antiperspirant and Deodorant**

   ▶ **Sunscreen**

   ▶ **Lotions and Moisturizers**

   ▶ **Cosmetics and Nail Polish**

Eco Fact

A 2008 study released by the EWG took a direct look at the amount of chemical exposure teen girls were experiencing from cosmetics and other personal care products. Through blood and urine samples of 20 girls aged 14 to 19, the EWG detected the presence of 16 chemicals from four chemical families, including phthalates, triclosan, parabens, and musks. These chemicals, including two parabens—methylparaben and propylparaben—were detected in every single girl tested.

Other studies have linked these ingredients to everything from an increased risk of cancer to hormone disruption. Other research suggests that teens, who use an average of 17 personal care products per day (as compared with the 12 used by adult women), are more sensitive to trace levels of hormone-disrupting chemicals because they are in a developmental phase.

TrueGreen: Monitoring Your Fluoride Levels

IF YOU'RE READY TO GO to the next level on your green journey, consider checking your household water's fluoride levels. While much of America's public water supply has been fluoridated since the 1940s, there is a rising concern that current levels are unhealthy for adults as well as children. Today, about 67 percent of the U.S. population on public water supplies has access to fluoridated water—it's what comes right out of our taps. In some areas of the country, such as Colorado, fluoride compounds are found naturally in the groundwater. In other areas, chemical fluoride ions are added to the drinking water supply.

The main goal of fluoridation is to keep our teeth healthy and white by warding off tooth decay. Still, information from the World Health Organization on tooth decay trends indicates that both fluoridated and unflouridated countries have seen a similar decline in tooth decay from the 1960s to the present.

While toxic at moderate to high doses, fluoride can be beneficial for dental health in low doses. The general level of fluoride in our water is supposed to range from 0.7–1.2 parts per million. The Environmental Protection Agency has also established a maximum contaminant level for human intake of fluoride, which is four milligrams per liter (mg/L), the legal limit of fluoride allowed in the water supply. But some estimates from 1992 suggested that approximately 1.4 million Americans had drinking water that included natural fluoride concentrations of 2.0–3.9 mg/L, and just over 200,000 people had concentrations equal to or exceeding 4 mg/L.

In 2006, the U.S. National Research Council took a hard look at the health risks associated with fluoride consumption and concluded that the EPA's current maximum contaminant level should be lowered to protect the general public. To date, this has not changed.

Overexposure to fluoride can cause bone weakening, kidney and reproductive damage, and endocrine disorders. Fluoride can also leach into groundwater and rivers, affecting the environment in various manners, from damaging pine forests to infiltrating salmon habitat and delaying migration.

While many people support the fluoridation of their local water supply, a growing number do not. You can protect yourself and your family from overexposure by monitoring your own household water. Most local water utilities supply a yearly water quality report; check with yours to determine your most recent fluoride levels. Some reports are available online at www.epa.gov/safewater/dwinfo/index.html.

There are also a number of water testing kits available online and through your local home supply store. If you find you do have elevated levels of fluoride, you can simply buy a filtering countertop pitcher or install the appropriate filter on your faucet or home water system.

SuperGreen:
Whipping Up Homemade Products

A FUN AND INEXPENSIVE way to green your personal care regimen is to create some of your own natural personal care and beauty products. While we've filed this activity under "SuperGreen," it can actually be a rather easy, entertaining, and gratifying process; you'll just need some extra time plus the right ingredients and a few clean jars and bottles. As with all personal care products, keep out of reach of children.

▶ **Deodorant: Mix 4 teaspoons alum (found in the spice section at the grocery store) with 2 teaspoons baking soda and 8 ounces of rubbing alcohol. Pour this mixture into a small spray bottle and use as a deodorant. A few drops of your favorite high-quality essential oil (peppermint, lavender, etc.) will add a fresh fragrance into the blend.**

You can create holistic beauty products right in your own kitchen. ©istockphoto.com/Rolf Weschke

▶ **Toothpaste: Mix 4 teaspoons of baking soda with ½ teaspoon water to get a good toothpaste consistency. Add 1 teaspoon salt and a few drops of flavoring (such as peppermint oil) to make the mixture pleasant to the taste. Store this mix at room temperature in an airtight container.**

▶ **Salt Glow Scrub: In a clean glass storage jar, mix together 4 ounces grapeseed oil, 2 ounces avacado oil, 1 tablespoon vitamin E oil, and 20 to 30 drops of your favorite high-quality essential oil (such as rosemary, lavender, eucalyptus, or sweet orange). Adding in just a few drops of rosemary oil will actually help preserve the shelf life. All of these ingredients are typically available at health food stores. Slowly blend 1 cup of sea salts into the oil blend. Store in a cool, dry place.**

▶ **Rose Water Toner: Toss one cup of fresh or dried rose buds and petals into a pot of water and bring to a boil. Turn the heat to medium and let your mixture simmer for 15 to 20 minutes. Let it cool a bit and pour the rose water into glass jars for storage. When almost completely cooled, place jars in the refrigerator to keep the rose water cold. You can use a funnel to pour this blend into a spray bottle for easy use as a fresh-smelling daily toner.**

Transportation is the second-largest source of CO_2 emissions in the U.S.

Week Seven: Green Your Transportation

T HE LURE OF THE OPEN ROAD. The bliss of independence. A sense of speed and power. A reliable mode of transport. With all the charisma surrounding our main form of transportation, it's no wonder Americans have long had a passion for the automobile. Some view their car as a purely utilitarian means of getting around, while others look to it as a four-wheeled representation of who they are.

Today, there are over 250 million cars in the U.S. and more than seven million cars are sold each year. A recent study by Experian Automotive of households with at least one automobile found that American households have an average of 2.28 vehicles. By comparison, the fast-growing auto market in China, which has a population of over 1.3 billion, only reported 22 million vehicles on the road in 2006. In fact, the world currently is home to about 625 million cars. The U.S.'s driving habits make it home to the largest passenger vehicle market in the world.

While our vehicles serve us well, they also contribute greatly to greenhouse gas emissions because most use gasoline, thus burning fossil fuels. The transportation sector in the U.S. is the second-largest source of CO_2 emissions for our country (with electricity generation as the first)—it was responsible for approximately 29 percent of total U.S. greenhouse gas emissions in 2006.

In this chapter, we'll take a look at why carbon emissions from vehicles matter so much and determine what budget-conscious changes we can all make to help reduce our carbon footprint. From fine-tuning our cars for optimum gas mileage to biking to work, there are a number of easy steps you can take to green your transportation—and even save some money in the meantime.

Why Carbon Emissions Matter

JUST 100 YEARS AGO IN the early 1900s, a very select group of Americans had only 8,000 cars—and only 144 miles of paved roads to drive them on. Things sure have changed in the last century. With more than 250 million vehicles traveling on four million miles of roads today, it is no wonder our country's emissions pack a punch.

Transportation is, in fact, the fastest-growing source of U.S. greenhouse gas emissions; it accounts for 47 percent of the country's increase in total emissions since 1990. CO_2 emissions, such as those produced by our prolific fleet of vehicles, are a greenhouse gas that contributes greatly to global warming.

As you likely know by now, climate change is the increase we are seeing in the average measured temperature of the Earth's surface air and oceans. From 1905 to 2005, this average temperature rose by 1.33 degrees Fahrenheit. The Intergovernmental Panel on Climate Change (IPCC) has concluded that this change is due to the increased levels of greenhouse gases in the atmosphere, the majority of which are due to human activities such as the generation of electricity and the use of gasoline for driving, both activities that burn fossil fuels.

When this excess of emissions reaches the atmosphere, they cause the "greenhouse effect," which is a process that involves the absorption and emission of infrared radiation by atmospheric gases. In the end, this event causes the temperature of the planet's lower atmosphere and surface to rise.

Through climate model projections, the IPCC predicts the average surface temperature of the earth will likely rise another 2 to 11.5 degrees Fahrenheit by the end of the 21st century. How will this affect the planet? As the heat gets turned up, the polar ice caps will continue to melt and cause sea levels to rise. An increase in the occurrence and intensity of extreme, unexpected weather events like Hurricane Katrina is also predicted. Significant changes in precipitation patterns will also come into play, changing more of the planet's landscape into desert. Other devastating issues can result from these changes, such as species extinction and the spread of disease.

The average car generates 4.5 tons of CO_2 emissions each year. ©istockphoto.com/matteo NATALE

Eco Fact

The effects of carbon emissions reach well beyond global warming, according to a study released in 2007 by a Stanford University scientist. Published in *Geophysical Research Letters* in 2008, the study revealed for the first time that increased levels of carbon dioxide in the atmosphere also lead to an increase in human mortality. Using a state-of-the-art computer model of the atmosphere that incorporated a vast number of physical and environmental chemical processes, the study found that for every one degree Celsius increase caused by carbon dioxide, the resulting air pollution would lead to approximately one thousand additional deaths plus many more cases of asthma and respiratory illness. Currently, it is estimated that there are about 20,000 deaths each year related to air pollution.

The World's Waning Oil Supply

AS THE WORLD'S POPULATION is expected to increase, so is its passion for the power of the automobile. By 2030, an estimated 1.2 billion cars will be on roads around the world. If gasoline continues to be the main source of fueling this fleet, the planet's drivers will nearly double the amount of carbon emissions that are sent into the atmosphere. One can only imagine the devastating climate-related effects of this trend.

Global warming aside, there is also concern regarding the world's remaining store of oil, from which gasoline is made. As a fossil fuel that is the product of compression and heating of ancient organic matter, oil is a non-renewable resource. At some point in time, it is highly likely that we will exhaust our global supply of oil, having burned it up in our vehicles and our homes' energy supplies.

The U.S. consumes over 20 million barrels of oil each day. ©istockphoto.com/egdigital

Many experts believe that the world will reach a point of "peak oil" production, after which supplies will begin to decline—just as demand via developing countries and population growth continues to rise.

While an International Energy Agency (IEA) report in late 2008 assuaged fears about peak oil, saying it would not occur at least until 2030, a large number of scientists believe this day of reckoning has already come and that oil supplies are currently in decline. Underscoring this belief is the fact that world oil production growth trends were flat from 2005 to 2008. The average yearly gains in global oil supply showed an increase of 1.2 million barrels per day from 1987 to 2005. But, according to another IEA Report, global production averaged 85.24 million barrels per day in 2006, up only .76 million barrels per day from 2005.

At the same time, oil consumption is expected to increase to 98.3 million barrels a day by 2015 and 118 million barrels per day by 2030. For the simple math to work out in favor of maintaining the world's demand for oil, production would have to increase by over 35 percent by 2030.

A dwindling supply and increasing demand from population growth and the automotive awakening of countries like India and China could cause the price of gasoline, already tipping upwards, to spike in the coming years. There is also speculation that, as supplies decline, those nations producing the oil will become more protective of their own supplies for their own citizens' use. Currently, the U.S. is the largest consumer of oil—we use over 20 million barrels per day but we only produced about 7.6 million barrels a day in 2005. Currently, over 50 percent of America's oil is imported from other countries. While there is a push to open up offshore drilling and search for new reserves, some experts believe that U.S. oil production peaked in 1970.

Eco Fact

As the world searches for additional stores of what it needs, a few new oil fields have come into the spotlight. One of these is a petroleum pool in the Gulf of Mexico that could increase the United States' reserves by more than 50 percent. This oil store lies 5.3 miles beneath the ocean surface, making it difficult to tap. As such, it will take several years and billions of dollars to get the job done. It is estimated this field could contain between three and 15 billion barrels of oil. The U.S. uses approximately 5.7 billion barrels of crude oil each year.

Driving for Better Gas Mileage

UNTIL ALTERNATIVE fuels and greener vehicles are developed for the mass market in this country, we can all help reduce our dependence on foreign oil, build up oil reserves, and reduce greenhouse gas emissions by employing a few simple fixes to our vehicles and our driving habits.

It is estimated that if each of us could get just three more miles per gallon out of our vehicles, the U.S. as a whole could save one million barrels of oil each day. It is also those vehicles with poor gas mileage that contribute the most to carbon emissions and global warming. For instance, a Dodge Durango SUV (with a 5.9 liter engine) gets about 12 miles per gallon in the city and emits an estimated 800 pounds of carbon dioxide over a distance of 500 city miles, according to the Environmental Protection Agency (EPA) 2000 Fuel Economy Guide. Alternatively, a Honda Insight that gets 61 mpg will only emit approximately 161 pounds of CO_2 in the same distance covered.

Obeying the speed limit could save you nearly 25 percent on your gas bills. ©istockphoto.com/David Birkbeck

Cost Meter: $0

One of the simplest ways to up your mpg is to drive more efficiently. This switch is not only cost-free, it will also save you money by shaving dollars off your monthly gasoline bills. The following tips, supplied by the EPA's fuel economy website (www.fueleconomy.gov) could lead you to save $1 or more on each and every gallon you use:

▶ **Driving Sensibly:** While it may be tempting at times, driving aggressively only costs you money (and spews extra emissions into the atmosphere). Avoiding driving habits like rapid acceleration and braking plus speeding could raise your gas mileage by 33 percent on the highway and 5 percent in the city.

▶ **Observing the Speed Limit:** Each vehicle reaches its optimal fuel economy at a certain speed but, in general, fuel economy decreases rapidly at speeds above 60 miles per hour. A general belief is that each 5 mph driven over 60 mph costs an additional 7 to 23 percent.

▶ **Just Say "No" to Idling:** Turn off the car if you're not inside or about to depart or end your trip. Idling gets zero miles per gallon, so your savings could be significant.

▶ **Cruising Right:** Using the cruise control, which helps maintain a consistent speed, and overdrive gears, which slows down the engine's speed, at appropriate times could also save a significant amount of fuel.

What are hypermilers? In the face of rising gas prices, this fringe group of drivers, who employ some unusual tactics to eek out their vehicle's ultimate gas mileage, has emerged. While not necessarily legal and not always safe, the techniques employed by hypermilers include minimizing braking, drafting freight trucks, and using downhills to gain added momentum for uphills. Some estimate they can achieve up to 50 mpg and more in average vehicles (i.e., non-hybrid) by hypermiling. In 2008, "hypermiling" was chosen as the word of the year by New Oxford American Dictionary. While these actions aren't recommended, perhaps this gas-saving group can inspire you to consider some of the suggestions in this chapter that will up your own mpg.

Fine-Tuning for Better Gas Mileage

IN ADDITION TO BEING conscious about the way you drive, a few key vehicle adjustments can help you obtain even better gas mileage on the road. Most of these suggestions are cost-free—even maintaining your vehicle properly is likely something you'd be doing anyway. Taking action keeps you in the driver's seat, all while helping to save the planet and a little bit of cash.

▶ **Removing Excess Weight:** If you have heavy items stashed in your car, stow them in the garage instead and, as a result, you could up your miles per gallon by another 1 to 2 percent (for 100 pounds). If you don't use them, removing the ski, bike, or cargo racks atop your vehicle could lighten the load and reduce drag.

Cost Meter: **$** to **$$**
(these changes will save you money)

Proper tire pressure can save you money at the pump.
©istockphoto.com/pixhook

▶ **Inflating Appropriately:** Keeping your tires properly inflated could increase the gas mileage you obtain by over 3 percent. Check your owner's manual for the right psi for your vehicle; this information is also typically located inside the driver's side door. If you have put new or different tires on your auto since its purchase, consult with the tire manufacturer for the proper psi. The EPA estimates that under-inflated tires can lower gas mileage by 0.3 percent for every one psi drop in pressure in all four tires.

▶ **Choosing the Right Fuel:** You can also check your owner's manual for the recommended octane level for your car; filling up with the right stuff will actually help increase your fuel efficiency.

Buying a higher-than-recommended octane level is usually a futile place to put your money, unless your engine is knocking. Additionally, drivers can amp up their mpg by 1 to 2 percent by using the manufacturer's recommended grade of motor oil.

▶ **Maintaining Your Vehicle:** Keeping your engine properly tuned is not only good for the longevity of your four-wheeled investment, it can also amp up the miles per gallon you obtain on a daily basis. According to the EPA, righting a critical maintenance issue like a faulty oxygen sensor could improve your mileage by as much as 40 percent and replacing a clogged air filter could up it by about 10 percent.

Considering Alternative Modes of Transportation

WHILE BUFFING UP your gas mileage via conscious driving techniques and the fine-tuning of your vehicle will certainly help keep untold amounts of emissions out of the atmosphere, the simple fact is that driving still uses up and burns oil. The average American drives over 33 miles each day.

Today, there are a variety of other commuting modes that can also help stall your emissions and conserve the dwindling non-renewable resource of oil. Could you carpool one or two days a week to work? Perhaps your company

would see clear to allow you to telecommute from home occasionally. If not, could you jump on the train or bus to reduce the number of miles your car is driven?

Better yet, you could lower your carbon footprint significantly—and add fitness and fun into your daily routine—if you choose to bike to work once in a while. Some people even choose to walk to work. In 2005, a study conducted by the Federal Highway Administration found that 107.4 million Americans use walking as a regular mode of travel.

Telecommuting

As the high cost of gas intermingles with the hassles of a time-consuming commute into the office, more and more workers are finding ways to work from home. In 2008, an estimated 100 million people worldwide did their jobs from home at least one day a month. In the U.S. alone, the 2008 projections stacked up to just under 40 million teleworkers—that equates to about 23 percent of the American workforce.

This trend has been on an upward trajectory since 1998, when about 10 million U.S. employees and just under 25 million workers worldwide spent one day a month getting their jobs done from home. The proliferation of fast broadband Internet connections, available everywhere from the coffee shop to the home, has made it easier than ever to work remotely.

If applicable to your line of work, check in with your employer to see if they offer a work-at-home program where you could telecommute anywhere from one day a month to a few days a week. In the U.S., the federal government, as well as some states, has even passed legislation to encourage more telecommuting. The Small Business Administration plans to develop a $5 million, four-year pilot program to encourage small businesses to allow telecommuting.

Cost Meter: $0
(this change will save you money)

Your home office expenses could even rate as a tax deduction, a fact that could save you even more money down the road. There is no question that this work mode is a trend on the rise. In fact, a 2008 report by research firm IDC predicts that almost 75 percent of the U.S. workforce will be mobile by 2011.

If teleworking is in your future, you'll be amazed at just how productive you can be when you're out of the office—you'll gain back the time spent in the car during your normal commute and you just might find you are even more efficient working at home.

Working at home can save you time and diminish your emissions. ©istockphoto.com/Dean Turner

Eco Fact

While the federal government holds out on making any wide-sweeping changes to regulate greenhouse emissions, some state and local governments are taking steps to set their own standards. In 2007, the governors of Arizona, California, New Mexico, Oregon, and Washington signed an agreement establishing the Western Climate Initiative, a combined effort to address climate change by reducing greenhouse gas emissions. Utah, the Canadian Provinces of Manitoba and British Columbia, and one Mexican state have also joined the initiative since its inception. The Initiative's regional greenhouse gas emissions reduction goal is to obtain a level that is 15 percent below 2005 levels by 2020.

Carpooling and Hopping on Public Transit

Sharing your ride with others in one form or another is a sure-fire way to lower your CO_2 emissions and save on your monthly gasoline bill. In fact, a study conducted by the American Public Transportation Association (APTA) found that families using public transportation could shave $6,200 annually off their transportation costs. The money saved could easily equate to one luxurious eco vacation.

About 14 million people use public transit daily and the APTA also suggests that public transit in America saves an astounding 1.4 billion gallons of gasoline yearly; it also keeps about 1.5 million tons of CO_2 from being emitted.

How can you jump into this positive cycle? If you drive to work every day, perhaps you could think outside the box and try out your local transit system. You can check for the availability of public transportation systems near you by logging onto www.publictransportation.org/systems or http://www.apta.com/links/state_local.

Cost Meter: $0
(this change will save you money)

People using public transit currently reduce CO_2 emissions by 1.5 million tons each year.
©istockphoto.com/David H. Lewis

Carpooling is another truly green way to travel. Whether you're driving to work or heading to a baseball game, the more people you can pack safely into the car, the lower each person's carbon footprint will be. You'll be sharing the ride, the emissions, and the cost of the trip. In fact it is estimated that carpooling saves the average commuter as much as $3,000 in vehicle costs each year.

It could also be a more efficient and speedier way to go if you travel on roads that have a high-occupancy vehicle (HOV) lane, which is usually a faster lane because it typically requires two or more people in each vehicle and there are, thus, fewer cars. In 2005, an ABC News poll found that only 8 percent of commuters were carpooling, but 20 percent of solo drivers say they would be interested in it. Why don't more people carpool? Convenience and the inability to link up with other local commuters are the main reasons.

Green Idea

Which states have the highest percentage of workers who carpool? Likely due to its higher gas prices, tropical Hawaii boasts a carpooling population of approximately 16.4 percent of all workers. Interestingly, Arizona (14.4 percent), Alaska (13.8 percent), and Utah (13.6 percent) rank second, third, and fourth, respectively. Which U.S. state came in last? Massachusetts, with only 7.2 percent of workers sharing their ride, possibly because many have chosen to take advantage of this state's strong public transit system.

Green Idea

Want to know how your mpg-savings efforts stack up? Compare your gas mileage with the optimum mileage obtainable for your vehicle at the EPA's fuel economy website www.fueleconomy.gov/mpg/MPG.do?action=garage.

With more and more people interested in greening their commute, it's no surprise that a few carpooling websites have launched to connect drivers. One is www.icarpool.com, which is a free carpooler connecting service that also enables you to track your monetary and CO_2 savings made through carpooling.

Carpooling is a sure-fire way to reduce your carbon footprint. ©istockphoto.com/Thania Navarro

Biking to Work

Beyond telecommuting and walking, there is perhaps no greener means of getting to work than commuting by bike. In fact, a recent assessment of the emissions produced from various commuting modes by the Sightline Institute found that cycling produced less than one-tenth of a pound of CO_2 per passenger mile. In comparison, a solo SUV driver's vehicle spits out almost two pounds, a rail transit with 25 riders per car is responsible for six-tenths of a pound, and a carpool vehicle with three occupants emits just over four-tenths of a pound.

Eco Fact

There are numerous bicycle-friendly communities across the country— these areas work to provide bike lanes and other amenities to cyclists to encourage travel by bike. To see if your city or town is bike-friendly, check out www.bicyclefriendlycommunity.org/ AllBicycleFriendlyCommunities.htm or www.bikeleague.org/programs/ bicyclefriendlyamerica/communities. In addition, the federal government has upped its yearly investment in improving conditions for bicycling from \$4.9 million in 1988 to \$416 million in 2002.

Cost Meter: **\$\$** to **\$\$\$\$**
(over time, a bike purchased for commuting will pay for itself)

Biking to work is both healthy and green.
©istockphoto.com/Rasmus Rasmussen

In addition to making your travel to work more earth-friendly, your bike commute will also serve as exercise and time outside, both valuable activities. A 2005 study by the Foundation for Environmental Conservation suggests that, instead of driving, biking to work or to run errands during each American's recommended dose of daily exercise could reduce the U.S.'s oil consumption by up to 38 percent. Since America produces such a large amount of the world's greenhouse gas emissions and 65 percent of adults are either overweight or obese, cycling to work could solve two significant problems.

How many people bike to work? According to the U.S. Census, in 1990 the percentage of journeys to work by bicycle was .41 percent (or, 466,856 people); in 2000, the percentage dropped slightly to .38 percent (or, 488,497 people). But, due to the green movement, bike commuting is on the rise—in 2006, the U.S. Census reported that participation grew to .50 percent. If spinning on the way to and from the work-place sounds like your cup of tea, check out these beginner tips from the League of American Bicyclists:

▶ **Choose a quality bike that is light enough for your needs; options include road or mountain bikes, hybrids, and touring bikes. Keep it maintained and the tires properly inflated.**

▶ **For short routes, wear your work clothing, but for longer ones, consider wearing proper clothing that can breathe and wick sweat, such as wool or Coolmax. Be sure to wear a helmet.**

▶ **Look for routes that minimize your need to deal with busy traffic; those with bike lanes are ideal. Be sure to follow all the road rules for signals and signs—safety is your priority.**

▶ **Lock your bike to an immovable object in a highly visible area out of the elements.**

▶ **Be sure to consider the weather patterns for the day and bring rain gear or warmer clothing if needed.**

For more detailed information on cycling to work, go to www.bikeleague.org/resources/better/commuters.php. Additionally, an easy way to see if biking to work is for you is to borrow or rent a bike and check out national Bike to Work Day, held yearly in May by the League of American Bicyclists.

Green Idea

One group, led by climate change expert Bill McKibben, is calling for an exact regulation on the effects of the world's emissions. This organization, 350.org, is spreading the scientifically proven word that 350 parts per million of carbon dioxide in the atmosphere is the safe bottom line for the planet.

Green Review: Things to Do During Week Seven

1. Try out driving smarter for better gas mileage using the following tactics and track your gas mileage to see the savings in action:

   ▶ **Drive sensibly, avoiding costly habits like speeding plus rapid acceleration and braking.**

   ▶ **Observe the speed limit to realize optimal fuel economy.**

   ▶ **Say "No" to idling and turn off the car if you're not inside it or about to depart or end your trip.**

   ▶ **Use your cruise control (to help maintain a consistent speed) and the overdrive gears (to slow down the engine's speed) at appropriate times.**

2. Fine-tune your vehicle to help realize better gas mileage and produce fewer emissions. Determine which of the following applies to you and put your plan into action:

   ▶ **Remove any unneeded excess weight from your auto.**

   ▶ **Inflate your tires to the psi recommended by the manufacturer of your vehicle.**

   ▶ **Choose the right fuel level, as recommended in your owner's manual.**

   ▶ **Perform any necessary maintenance to properly tune up your car or truck or make some time to do the work yourself if you know how.**

3. Consider if you can use an alternate, greener mode to commute to work and test it out for a day:

   ▶ **Telecommuting**

   ▶ **Public transit**

   ▶ **Carpooling**

   ▶ **Biking to work**

©istockphoto.com/ Konstantinos Kokkinis

TrueGreen: Offsetting Your Emissions

IF YOU'D LIKE TO TAKE the next step along your journey to go green, buying a carbon pass or credits to offset your emissions will buy you some peace of mind and also help support projects that aim to dissipate the effects of increasing greenhouse gases in the earth's atmosphere. Carbon offsets offer drivers (and all consumers of emissions-causing activity) the opportunity to displace the CO_2 they produce by supporting projects such as those that develop renewable energy, promote energy efficiency, and support reforestation.

The goal with carbon offsets is to use them as a way to further help the planet after you've done all you can do to reduce your own emissions—not to justify CO_2-producing behavior. Critics of offsets voice concerns that these credits simply postpone real solutions. So, be sure to employ the greener strategies that are applicable to your life and supplement this commitment with offsets.

A key question to ask when shopping for a carbon offsetting service is if the provider is "verified." The popularity of offsetting has led to the rise of a plethora of provider options, but not all are trusted sources. Since you are buying an intangible item, be sure to do a little homework before you buy.

Look for verified offset providers such as Native Energy (www.nativeeneregy.com), the Conservation Fund (www.conservationfund.org), www.terrapass.com, or www.e-BlueHorizons.com.

Carbon offsets support projects such as the development of renewable energy and reforestation.
©istockphoto.com/René Mansi

These companies enable you to calculate your own personal CO_2 emissions from driving (or other activities) directly on their websites so you can add up your own impact. A good place to compare and contrast the details, from costs to project types and certification/verification, of some of the key carbon offset providers is at http://www.ecobusinesslinks.com/carbon_offset_wind_credits_carbon_reduction.htm.

The cost of carbon credits start at about $36 to offset the yearly emissions of a small car and range upwards depending on your energy use. A study done in 2007 found that offset prices ranged from $1.80 to $300 per ton of emissions, with most coming in around $6 a ton. Since the prices are so varied, it may pay to shop around for the best deal and the most trusted provider.

SuperGreen: Buying a Fuel-Efficient Vehicle

ARE YOU IN THE MARKET for a new vehicle? If so, there is no better time to take a larger step for the health of the planet and choose a fuel-efficient vehicle. As you might imagine, this move will also save you a significant amount of money on yearly fuel bills.

The fuel-efficient Mini Cooper gets 32 mpg on the highway. ©istockphoto.com/Mathew Dixon

The best place to conduct your green vehicle research is at the EPA's Green Vehicle Guide, which is online at www.epa.gov/greenvehicles. Here, you can research the best options in the state where you live and plan to purchase your vehicle. The guide helps consumers choose the cleanest and most efficient vehicles to meet their needs; it actually rates cars and trucks from the past nine years according to their emissions and fuel economy. Rating categories include Air Pollution Score, Greenhouse Gas Score, and Fuel Economy.

As an example, the EPA's guide states that a 2009 Honda Civic automatic five-speed vehicle (1.8L/4 cylinder) gets 36 miles to the gallon on the highway and 25 mpg in the city. It achieves an Air Pollution score of 6 out of 10 and a Greenhouse Gas Score of 8 out of 10. On the flip side, a 2009 Mercury Mountaineer automatic 4WD vehicle (4L/6 cylinder) gets 13 mpg in the city and 19 on the highway. It achieves an Air Pollution score of 7 and a Greenhouse Gas score of 2.

The EPA also gives qualifying vehicles a SmartWay or SmartWay Elite designation; this indicates these choices are particularly earth-friendly.

To fall into the SmartWay designation, vehicles must achieve a score of 6 or better in both the Air Pollution and Greenhouse Gas categories plus achieve a combined score of at least 13 when added together. To attain the SmartWay Elite designation, vehicles must score a 9 or better on both categories.

Hybrid vehicles, which are vehicles powered by two or more distinct sources (i.e., gas and a rechargeable energy storage system) are another extremely fuel-efficient option. These are also included in the EPA guide and may be somewhat more expensive than other fuel-efficient vehicles, such as a Honda Civic or Toyota Yaris, but they are probably the most gas-saving option beyond an electric car. When calculating your budget for a new car purchase, figure in the money you'll save on gas over the years it's owned, and you may find that a hybrid vehicle purchase becomes more plausible.

Travelers can easily make their trips more earth-conscious.

©istockphoto.com/One Mean Pixel

Week Eight: Green Your Travel

SINCE THE DAWN OF THE STEAMSHIP and the advent of the airplane, world travel has always appealed to the senses. The act of jetting off to a faraway escape is infused with exoticism, romance, and adventure. Even domestic and regional sojourns help us escape the everyday doldrums and stresses of life.

Thus, it is no surprise that the travel and tourism machine is the world's largest business—travelers drop a whopping two to three trillion dollars on trips annually. According to a Travel Industry Association (TIA) survey, Americans alone took nearly two million domestic trips in 2005, including those for business and pleasure.

Like the rest of the world's transportation, however, travel takes a heavy toll on the planet. For instance, air travel is one of the biggest fuel-guzzling forms of transport. In fact, the United Nation's Intergovernmental Panel on Climate Change estimates that aviation is responsible for a full 3.5 percent of global warming; it also suggests that this figure could rise to a concerning 15 percent by 2050.

Fear not, as you don't have to give up all those stress-free vacations— you simply have to alter your plans a bit to green your travel. In the end, traveling with the planet in mind will also greatly enhance the quality of your journey.

This chapter reviews just how travel taxes the planet and outlines the simple steps you can take and the choices you can make to reduce your own impact when on the road (or in the air) for business or pleasure. In turn, many of your eco-conscious decisions will also serve as those that help keep your budget intact.

How Does Travel Tax the Planet?

UNLESS YOUR TRAVEL PLANS involve driving an electric car, cycling, or walking to your destination, emissions are always created via our means of transportation, whether they be automobile, cruise ship, or airplane. Air travel is one of the biggest greenhouse gas offenders due to the amount of fuel required to fly today's airplanes. A jet with average occupancy is responsible for almost as many pounds of CO_2 emissions per passenger per mile as the average car driven by a single occupant.

The proliferation of air travel today compounds this problem. According to the National Air Traffic Controllers Association, on an average day, air traffic controllers oversee 28,537 commercial flights plus 27,178 private flights, 24,548 air taxi flights (planes for hire), 5,260 military flights, and 2,148 air cargo flights. This adds up to over 87,000 flights per day, 64 million takeoffs and landings per year, and untold amounts of climate-changing emissions.

In addition to CO_2, which has the same amount of climate effect no matter where it is spewed into the atmosphere, scientists suggest that other aircraft emissions like nitrogen oxides have serious climate effects because of the elevation at which they are injected into the atmosphere. In the short term, these emissions have more than double the effects of CO_2 alone. They will, however, eventually dissipate while carbon dioxide remains effective for decades.

Some experts also suggest that contrails, the high-altitude vapor trails created by aircraft when water vapor freezes around particles of engine exhaust, also play a role in climate change. This theory was put to the test during the three days following the tragic events of September 11th, 2001, when all American air traffic was grounded. Researchers discovered that the absence of contrails expanded the difference between daytime and nighttime temperatures by a full degree Celsius when compared with the average recorded during the last three decades.

This recorded difference was even greater in air-traffic-heavy, mid-latitude regions of the planet. These results indicate that contrails dampen natural temperature variations. A 2004 NASA study added more light to the scenario; it predicted that contrails alone will increase temperatures in the lower atmosphere of the U.S. by at least one degree every 20 years.

Over 87,000 flights take to the skies in the U.S. each day. ©istockphoto.com/Mark Evans

Eco Fact

Airports themselves are also considerable polluters of local air quality. Airplanes give off huge amounts of exhaust fumes during taxiing, takeoff, and landing. According to the National Resource Defense Council's *Flying Off Course* report, many airports across the country are among the top ten polluters in their city.

As the burgeoning business of travel and tourism continues to grow—the United Nations' World Travel Organization (UNWTO) projects an average of 4 percent growth per year—so will the resulting emissions and their climate effects. The impact could be significant, given the fact that the average commercial flight in the U.S. releases nearly 1,800 pounds of greenhouse gases per passenger into the atmosphere, according to the Edinburgh Centre for Carbon Management.

Travelers' yearly pilgrimages to the ocean can amount to tons of emissions. ©istockphoto.com/John Zellmer

In addition to issues with emissions, air travel also requires the use of fossil fuels, which we know are a waning non-renewable resource. In 1960, there were 2,135 certificated air carrier airplanes in the U.S. that consumed almost two billion gallons of fuel. Today, there are over 8,000 aircraft using more than 13.5 billion gallons of jet fuel annually. Additionally, the UNWTO predicts that there will be 1.6 billion international tourist "arrivals" (i.e., trips) worldwide by 2020.

Are cleaner aircraft fuels on the horizon? Hydrogen fuel cells have been touted as a greener, potentially viable alternative fuel for airplanes, but the development of this fuel and its supporting technologies is still in its infancy. The world's first hydrogen-fuel-cell-only-powered plane did take to the skies, however, in October of 2008 in Germany. While this accomplishment signals a groundbreaking point in hydrogen fuel cell technology, there is still a very long way to go before it could be used for commercial flights; some experts estimate a lead time of at least 30 years.

In the meantime, some airlines are being targeted to claim responsibility for their emissions. A 2008 ruling by the European Union (EU) places a cap on allowed emissions and requires all airlines arriving at or leaving from airports in the EU to purchase pollution credits beyond those amounts. This new environmental policy will begin in 2012 and will affect a number of U.S. carriers.

Beyond travel transportation emissions, tourism can also tax the planet by treading heavily on local environments, especially those that are fragile or protected. Conscious touring is the green way to go when you head out the door for a much-needed vacation or some quick business travel. The next few pages will deliver a few tips, tricks, and ideas to help get you on a more eco-friendly path when it comes to traveling.

Considering a Staycation

SKYROCKETING GAS PRICES and the fallout of recessionary times during 2008 launched a fevered interest in the phenomenon of "staycationing"—taking a vacation while staying at home and relaxing or taking day trips in the area. In fact, a recent survey conducted by TIA and Ypartnership, a travel research firm, found that 14 percent of vacationers had taken a staycation while another 9 percent were planning one.

Thinking out of the box, about 22 percent of staycationers in the TIA survey (5.1 million adults) said they planned to spend at least one night in a hotel, motel, or resort during their time off work. Mix it up to suit your preferences and experience a restful, rejuvenating vacation.

If camping out in the backyard isn't appealing, you can still pack an eco punch by choosing to take a trip within your region. In fact, it seems most travelers prefer short trips, many of which are taken locally. The 2005 TIA Travel Market Overview found that 51 percent of travelers took day trips while 29 percent spent only one to two nights away from home. If your trip is done solo (like 36 percent of those taken in 2005), it will not be as eco-friendly as a vacation taken with several people—the more the greener.

Cost Meter: $0
(this change will save you money)

What are some ways you can forego the costs and stresses associated with a travel vacation and realize a fun and frugal staycation?

▶ **Plan to "get away:" Turn off all work-related electronics, such as your computer, and hide them away or, better yet, give them to a friend for the week. This will also help reduce your energy consumption for the week.**

▶ **Avoid any chores: Hire a housekeeper to clean up after you during the week; the extra cost will be marginal compared to your vacation savings. If you'd prefer not to cook, order in your meals and check out new or favorite restaurants around town.**

▶ **Plan some activities: Beyond pure relaxing, embarking on a few pre-determined activities could make your staycation feel more like a vacation. Does your area have a special attraction (i.e., museums, national parks, a great hiking trail) you've always wanted to check out? Where do tourists go when they come to your area? Now is the time to take advantage of what you've got.**

▶ **Get in the mode: Be sure to do things you'd normally do while on vacation—take photos, splurge on that decadent dessert, buy a nice bottle of wine, stay up late, and sleep in.**

Embracing Slow Travel

H OW OFTEN HAVE YOU come back from a weeklong vacation only to feel as if you need to go on another to recover from the travel whirlwind you just endured? The concept of slow travel seeks to soothe travelers' souls with a more restful, simple vacation that is based in one spot for a longer time.

Instead of focusing on covering all the high points of an area, it's all about savoring the day-to-day delights of one location, including its local people, shops, culture, and food. Instead of trying to hit all the "must-see" tourist attractions of Italy in one or two weeks, for instance, slow travelers opt to check into a villa in the wine country for that timeframe and relish the beauty of the place, its fruit of the vine, and the local culture.

Plant yourself in a seaside villa and soak up the view and the local culture—slowly. ©istockphoto.com/Daniel Breckwoldt

Cost Meter: $0
(this change will save you money)

The slow travel movement is an offshoot of the slow food movement, which was born in Italy as a protest in the 1980s when McDonald's opened in Rome. The tenets of slow food include preserving regional cuisine, local farming, and traditional food preparation methods. Like slow food's connection to local cuisine, slow travel provides a connection to local peoples and cultures.

Because it involves fewer transportation requirements, slow travel is a simple, smart choice for the environment—and your wallet. It can also deliver a richer, more memorable experience. To join in this growing travel trend, consider booking an apartment, a cottage, or villa or looking into a house swap in an area you'd like to explore. A few resources for information include:

▶ **www.slowplanet.com**

▶ **www.slowtrav.com**

▶ **www.slowtraveltours.com**

Choosing Ecotourism

A S A FORM OF tourism that is attractive to eco-conscious and socially conscious travelers, ecotourism focuses on responsible travel to natural areas. The "responsible" part of that formula equates to preserving the local environment and improving the well-being of the local people.

True ecotourism programs minimize the negative aspects associated with conventional travel—it encourages earth-friendly tactics such as recycling plus energy and water conservation. It also promotes bolstering the health of local economies with ecotourism travel dollars.

Cost Meter: **$$$** to **$$$$**

Ecotourism is growing three times faster than the tourism industry itself. ©istockphoto.com/Peter Malsbury

According to the International Ecotourism Society (TIES), ecotourism aims to do the following:

1. Minimize impact

2. Build environmental and cultural awareness and respect

3. Provide positive experiences for both visitors and hosts

4. Provide direct financial benefits for conservation

5. Provide financial benefits and empowerment for local people

6. Raise sensitivity to the host countries political, environmental, and social climate

Green on the Cheap

To find a less costly stateside ecotourism vacation, check out the following states' ecotourism societies:

• **Alaska:** Alaska Wilderness Recreation & Tourism Association; www.awrta.org

• **Arizona:** La Ruta de Sonora Ecotourism Association; www.laruta.org

• **Hawaii:** Hawaii Ecotourism Association; www.hawaiiecotourism.org

• **Wisconsin:** Travel Green Wisconsin (a program that encourages hotels and tour operators to reduce their environmental impact); www.travelgreenwisconsin.com

The lure of ecotourism is strong today, especially with those who are concerned about the health of the planet. In fact, a 2003 survey found that three-quarters of U.S. travelers "feel it is important their visits not damage the environment."

According to TIES, ecotourism has been growing since the 1990s at a rate of 20 to 34 percent a year—by 2004 it was growing three times faster globally than the tourism industry itself. In the U.S., about 13 percent of the 18.6 million outbound leisure travelers (about 2.4 million Americans) are considered ecotourists.

While ecotourism is often equated with visiting exotic locales such as Costa Rica, Africa, Nepal, and Bhutan, ecotourism does exist right here in the U.S. In fact, it is estimated that there are 900 million visits per year on domestic federal lands to pristine places like national forests, national parks, monuments, wildlife refuges, and preserves. Traveling across the globe to experience an ecotourism locale can be a more costly (but worthwhile and life-enhancing) endeavor. If you're looking to keep a solid handle on your budget, research ecotourism opportunities that exist on American soil or sea.

The TIES website, www.ecotourism.org, is an excellent place to start when searching for ecotourism operators. Another resource is www.ecotour.com. Greenwashing, which is the false use or overstatement of eco-conscious policies, also exists in this industry so be sure to do some background research and book with a reputable provider.

Supporting Green Businesses When You Travel

PUTTING YOUR greenbacks where your green commitment lies will help support those businesses making earth-friendly choices and encourage the future growth of eco-friendly travel options. There hasn't been a better time to travel green—there are more eco-friendly hotels, lodges, ski resorts, music festivals, and even green airlines than ever before.

In the air, Costa Rica's NatureAir is the first carbon-neutral airline; it voluntarily compensates for its emissions with offsets that go toward tropical forest conservation efforts in the country's Osa Peninsula. NatureAir donates money to local landowners there to keep the forest safe from clearcutting. The airline has also recently joined the United Nation's Climate Neutral Network, which promotes global action towards low-carbon economies and societies.

Booking a green hotel just might enable you to sleep better at night. ©istockphoto.com/Steven Miric

Cost Meter: **$** to **$$$**

Other airlines are still remiss to offset their massive emissions, but they offer consumers the opportunity to do so for themselves. For example, Continental Airlines launched a voluntary carbon offsetting program in 2007 that allows customers to view the carbon footprint of their booked itinerary and lets them make a contribution to Sustainable Travel International to fund the purchase of carbon offset credits. Delta Airlines was the first to offer its customers an offsetting option. Today, others including Northwest, American Airlines, Cathay Pacific, Virgin Blue, and SAS have similar programs. Virgin actually offers its passengers the option to purchase offsets from the aisle during flights.

On the ground, there is a movement afoot to build green hotels and convert others to boast more eco-conscious features. One example is the Hotel Terra in Jackson Hole, Wyoming, a boutique hotel opened in 2008 that has been built to LEED (Leadership in Energy and Environmental Design) certification specifications. Eco features include water conservation systems like low flow water fixtures, dual flush toilets, solar powered faucets in public restrooms, and native landscaping requiring no irrigation.

This slopeside hotel also boasts 100-percent recycled "Eco Shake" roof shingles and low VOC (volatile organic compounds) carpeting and paints for improved air quality. Many other lodging options across the country offer similar features. To search for green lodging go to www.greenlodge.org or www.environmentally friendlyhotels.com.

Even some ski resorts have a sustainable side.
©istockphoto.com/Ingmar wesemann

Eco Fact

Is your green vacation taking you to the beach? A 2008 settlement with the Natural Resources Defense Council (NRDC) will lead the U.S. Environmental Protection Agency (EPA) to update its 22-year-old criteria for reporting beach-related health hazards to the public. Currently, the EPA assesses ocean-water and beach health based on the likelihood of beachgoers contracting gastro-intestinal illnesses. The new and improved criteria, to be released by 2012, will include same-day reporting of the likelihood of visitors contracting skin rashes, hepatitis, pink eye, and ear infections. The NRDC says that there were over 22,000 pollution-related closures or warning advisories on U.S. beaches in 2007, mainly due to runoff and human and animal waste present in the water. To check the status of the beach that may be your destination, head to http://oaspub.epa.gov/beacon/beacon_national_page.main.

In addition to green airlines and hotels, there are a growing number of sustainable eco spas rising up across the country. Many of these day and resort spas focus on using organic, plant-based products for everything from facials to massages and body scrubs. Some also shine a spotlight on water conservation, green building and décor, and recycling efforts. Greener spas can be located on www.spafinder.com.

Earth consciousness is even cropping up in Sin City. Harrah's Entertainment is enabling guests to atone for their eco sins by purchasing carbon offsets via Native Energy, a high-quality provider that uses funds to support renewable energy projects. Harrah's, which operates Caesars and Horseshoe brand names, is also committed to energy conservation at its properties.

If concerts or music festivals are your idea of a solid vacation, you just might find that many have a green side. One example is the three-day Telluride Blues & Brews music festival, which is held each September in the shadow of the majestic Rocky Mountains in Telluride, CO.

Recycling and composting centers are set up near the food and beer tents to promote as little waste as possible. All vendors are required to use compostable plates, cups, and utensils. In addition, festival organizers also offer a Be Green Ticket upgrade for $2.50, which supports renewable energies such as wind and bio-energy and helps to offset about 340 pounds of CO_2.

For those who enjoy skiing and snowboarding or simply sidling up to the bar after skiing, it is easier than ever to choose to hit the slopes at an eco-conscious resort. It is perhaps in part their own vested interest in keeping global warming at bay (and keeping the powder on the hill) that has many mitigating their own emissions.

Eco-conscious trash removal packs a punch at a festival like Telluride Blues & Brews, which has nearly 8,000 attendees. ©Darren Croke

The National Ski Areas Association's Sustainable Slopes Annual Report reveals that 68 resorts are now purchasing clean energy for their operations via renewable energy credits. Of these resorts, 34 are offsetting 100 percent of their greenhouse gas emissions. As a whole, these earth-conscious resorts are purchasing enough kilowatts of green power annually to account for almost 5.5 million pounds of carbon dioxide emissions.

Overall, when planning your travel, look for lodging, resorts, festivals, and events that also pay homage to the health of the planet. The money you spend there helps support these causes and enables them to proliferate.

Green on the Cheap

Even if you do nothing else, bringing reusable bags and bottles along for the ride when you head out on vacation wins you some serious green points. Use a stainless steel reusable bottle for portable water instead of the disposable plastic water bottles bought in the store. And, bringing a reusable grocery sack along with you every time you hit the market will save a significant number of plastic bags.

Green Review: Things to Do During Week Eight

1. When it comes time to plan your next vacation, consider taking a staycation right in your own home. To realize the maximum relaxation benefit from this type of sojourn, be sure to unplug computers, PDAs, and anything else that may tempt you to do some work.

2. If you have the travel bug and staying at home is not appealing, think about booking a slow travel vacation, where you and your family or friends check into a villa, condo, or home in one locale and explore and enjoy the local culture.

3. If you enjoy nature and believe in the concept of preserving local cultures and economies, consider an ecotourism vacation.

4. Whenever you travel for work or pleasure, whether it's a day trip or a month-long excursion, try to choose green businesses when you book things like lodging and airfare and select destinations like ski resorts, music festivals, and casinos.

5. Green your travel simply by packing a reusable bag and water bottle to help minimize your waste along the way, wherever you go.

©istockphoto.com/Duncan Walker

TrueGreen: Buying Carbon Offsets

UNLESS YOU PLAN A STAYCATION that truly keeps you nestled in your own home, any type of vacation or work trip taken will still use up resources like energy and water plus produce greenhouse gases—namely, climate-changing carbon emissions—from the fuel you burn while driving or flying to your destination. You may choose to tack on a few extra offsetting dollars here and there when the opportunity presents itself via airline and hotel bookings or ski lift and festival tickets, but it will take a real green commitment to actually sit down and determine your yearly travel emissions and take the steps to purchase carbon offsets.

Once you've done all you can to realistically reduce your travel emissions, the next step on your green journey would be to find a trusted offset provider and buy enough to help mitigate the effects of your travel. The purchase of offsets supports emissions-reducing projects such as the development of renewable energy, the promotion of energy efficiency, and reforestation.

For example, the Conservation Fund is one offset provider that supports reforestation projects. According to the company, an estimated 20 percent of global greenhouse gas emissions are caused by deforestation. Since 2000, the Conservation Fund's purchased offsets have restored over 20,000 acres of forestlands with six million trees through its carbon sequestration programs. It estimates that these trees will capture approximately 7.2 million tons of carbon dioxide from the atmosphere over their lifetime.

Costs range widely for offsets, so shopping around can save you some money. The research firm New Carbon Finance says that prices for consumer offsets climbed 26 percent from 2007 to 2008, from $5 to $6.32 per ton of greenhouse gas. The online travel site Travelocity offers carbon offset packages via the Conservation Fund at prices ranging from $3.42 per person for a one-day trip (which offsets almost one half a short ton of CO_2) to $8.29 per person for a seven-day trip that offsets just over a short ton of CO_2.

Some reliable sources for the purchase of carbon offsets include the Conservation Fund (www.conservationfund.org), Native Energy (www.nativeenergy.com), and TerraPass (www.terrapass.com).

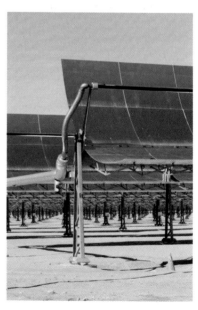

Offsetting your travel emissions can help support projects like solar power. ©istockphoto.com/MaxFX

SuperGreen: Booking a Volunteer Vacation

CONGRATULATIONS—you've journeyed through a full eight weeks of greening your lifestyle! How can you celebrate? Perhaps you can take all the money you've saved on everything from energy and water bills to transportation costs and book yourself an earth-friendly vacation, an eco spa weekend, or an ecotourism adventure.

If you'd like to go even further still in greening your life, a volunteer vacation that focuses on helping the planet or local peoples will certainly solidify your eco-conscious credibility. As concerns about the health of the planet rise, this type of travel is gaining in popularity. A recent TIA Voice of the Traveler study revealed that about one-quarter of travelers are interested in taking a volunteer or service-based vacation.

The theme of volunteer vacations that focus on the environment can range from planting trees in Guatemala and restoring coral reefs in places like Curacao and Antigua to working on an organic farm in Italy. One eco-conscious volunteer vacation example is an opportunity to help save the Costa Rican rainforest with United Planet, an international non-profit organization. Volunteers assist in protecting endangered macaws or preserving the rainforest biome through education and direct action.

Even though you'll be volunteering to help a cause, there will be costs associated with your vacation. The Charity Guide suggests that, while some projects pay a stipend to volunteers, most vacation program fees range from $50 to $3,000

because projects need to cover costs associated with recruiting, volunteer training, and on-site coordination. United Planet suggests that a one-week stay in the rainforest will cost volunteer vacationers about $1,395 plus their air travel and transportation. The nonprofit organizations you'll be helping to support use this money to provide food, lodging, and funding for the project on which you are working.

Some volunteer vacations offer more rustic accommodations (such as a tent in a national park) while others deliver more civilized lodging. A source for the latter is Global Volunteers (www.globalvolunteers.org), which also supplies hotel accommodations, prepared meals, and a volunteer coordinator.

Be sure to check with the volunteer vacation organization of your choice, as part or all of your program fees and travel expenses can be tax deductible. Other resources for volunteer vacations include www.wwoof.org and www.unitedplanet.org.

You can help save the world by planting trees while on vacation. ©istockphoto.com/ruchos

Kids and pets can also live healthier, more eco-friendly lives.

Extra Credit: Eco Kids and Green Pets

11

THE NUMEROUS TOXINS IN our world today also greatly affect our children and the pets we care for. If you happen to have kids or domesticated animals in your life, then this chapter is right up your alley.

According to the U.S. Census Bureau, the number of children under the age of 18 in the U.S. in 2006 was 73.7 million, a number that represents nearly 25 percent of the entire population of the country. Kids are a growing force—their numbers are up from 47.3 million in 1950. It is also anticipated that by 2030, their ranks will grow to 85.7 million.

Because children have smaller, developing systems and higher metabolisms, they can be much more vulnerable to the toxic effects of the various chemicals we have discussed in previous chapters. Everything from pesticides and insecticides to BPA and the chemicals present in personal care products can negatively affect the health of kids today.

When it comes to pets, their smaller systems also mean they bear a higher body burden of harmful chemicals. All domestic animals, including dogs, cats, and birds, can be affected by the chemicals present in everything from Teflon-coated pans to plastic toys and food.

This chapter takes a look at how you can make a major impact in the lives of your children, as well as those of your pets, by applying your green inclinations to various factors that can affect both. Because not everyone has children or pets, this chapter was not included in this book's eight-week plan, but this doesn't mean that the topic is any less important to address. In fact, for a variety of reasons, it could be even more critical.

Why Should Kids Be Green, Too?

CHILDREN LOOK TO THEIR parents and family for direction on shaping their own values and beliefs. When you share your views on why it is important to respect the planet and take care of it, you are helping to shape a lifelong eco-conscious commitment. A child who grows up recycling, eating local foods, and supporting alternative energy will likely become an adult who continues to do so.

Kids growing up today face an uncertain future filled with questions about global warming, peak oil, and the health effects of the chemicals present in our foods and water supply. Answering their earth-related questions patiently and honestly will help them face the challenges ahead with courage and intelligence.

You can also protect your children from the harmful chemicals present in our everyday lives. The choices you make at home in all the areas discussed in previous chapters—including choosing green cleaning products, buying organic foods, filtering drinking water, using natural personal care products—will have an even more serious impact on the health of your children than your own.

A 2005 study conducted by the Environmental Working Group (EWG) investigated the presence of industrial chemicals, pollutants, and pesticides by performing tests on the umbilical cord blood of newborn infants. This benchmark research focused on this area because the umbilical cord pulses the equivalent of 300 quarts of blood each day, including the nutrients needed for healthy growth, to the developing fetus.

As a result of the study, researchers found an average of 200 industrial chemicals and pollutants in blood samples from the 10 babies tested. The roundup included an alarming blend of pesticides, mercury, the possibly carcinogenic perfluorochemicals (PFCs) created by Teflon and Scotchgard products, and brain-development-hindering PBDEs from flame retardants in furniture and computers. Even wastes from burning coal, gasoline, and garbage were present.

These findings make it painfully apparent that the developing fetuses of pregnant women, which have incomplete defense systems and immature blood-brain barriers, are being fed a stream of chemicals and pollutants. Some scientists suggest that this type of exposure is leading to increasing rates of childhood cancers, autism, ADHD, and birth defects.

The future of the earth—and its population of children—is in your hands.
©istockphoto.com/Jani Bryson

As children grow up, they continue to be more susceptible than adults to the prevalence of toxic chemicals in our world. Their still-developing cells make them more vulnerable, especially to neurotoxins that affect the nervous system. They also take in more toxins per pound of body weight than adults and lay claim to immature immune systems that cannot adequately protect their bodies.

Making the right choices for your family at home and when traveling is the best move you can make to protect them—and the planet. While it may be easy to become overwhelmed with the possibilities of your children coming into contact with toxins, simply do the best you can and be sure to still let kids be kids.

Greening Your Children

From the moment they are conceived until they reach adulthood, children are extremely susceptible to modern life's barrage of chemicals and pollutants. The way they live as crawling infants, running toddlers, and fast-growing kids can lead them to greater exposure since they often put their hands in their mouths (and transfer every toxin they touch into their bodies) and play outside in dirt and grass that has likely been treated with harmful fertilizers, pesticides, and weed killers.

There are many ways you can help reduce the body burden of chemicals that your kids must bear. The next few sections offer some key tips for greening their lives and teaching them to love the planet.

In Utero: What to Avoid When You're Expecting

THE BEST TIME TO CLEAN up your home and your act from harmful chemicals is actually before you even become pregnant. There is no better example of this than the EWG study that revealed the prolific presence of toxins present in umbilical cord blood. Of the 287 chemicals detected, a full 180 are known to cause cancer in humans or animals, 217 are toxic to the brain and nervous system, and 208 have caused birth defects or abnormal development in animal tests.

Cost Meter: **$** to **$$$**

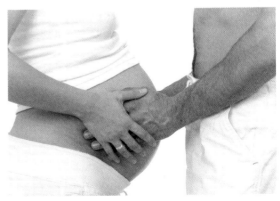

Is your baby safe from toxins? ©istockphoto.com/doram

Tossing the toxic cleaning supplies, losing the lawn fertilizers, pitching the pesticides in non-organic foods, and ditching the carcinogenic chemicals in personal care products will clean up your own health and prepare your body to be a safe haven for your child to be conceived and grow in. Once you are pregnant, you can rest easy knowing you've done all you can to give your baby a healthy start and a toxin-free home to be born into.

Many of these switches have been covered in previous chapters of this book, so if you've followed the eight-week plan laid out here, you've made great strides in preparing for pregnancy and beyond.

If you'd like to review this key information on cleaning up relevant areas of your life, head to the following:

▶ **Choosing natural cleaning products to clean up air quality: Chapter 3**

▶ **Buying pesticide-free organic foods and eating safer seafood: Chapter 5**

▶ **Using natural lawn care strategies to reduce pesticides and fertilizer exposure: Chapter 6**

▶ **Choosing natural personal care products to reduce chemical exposure: Chapter 8**

Eco Fact

Is your baby's bottle BPA-free? Growing concern about the potential health effects of bisphenol A (BPA) led the Canadian government to ban the sale of plastic baby bottles containing the chemical in 2008. The country's federal ministries of Health and the Environment moved after a report found that BPA, which is used to harden plastic and make it shatterproof, is a danger to people and particularly to newborns and infants. The biggest concerns with BPA are possible effects on reproductive development and hormone disruption. To date, the U.S. Food and Drug Administration and European Union maintain that BPA is safe for use in all applications, including baby bottles, polycarbonate water bottles, and food packaging for canned goods and soups. At the same time, the Center for Science in the Public Interest, a health-advocacy group, has warned that pregnant women should limit their exposure even to packaging that contains BPA to avoid passing it onto their unborn children. There are many safer baby bottle options today, including BPA-free versions from Green to Grow, Born Free, Medela, Adiri, and Thinkbaby. Old-fashioned glass bottles are also a safe option that has always been free of BPA.

Creating a Healthy Nursery or Bedroom

Cost Meter: **$$** to **$$$**

WHEN A BABY IS ON THE WAY, one of the first things expectant parents are inspired to do is decorate a nursery for their child-to-be. But if you're using products like conventional paints, carpeting, and wallpaper, you may just be doing your baby more harm than good. Whether remodeling for a precious new infant's nursery or redoing your child's bedroom, following a few green tips can help keep them healthy and happy in the long run. Opting for green home improvement products may cost you a little bit more, but they will more than pay for themselves in peace of mind.

▶ **Paint Clean:** Blue for a boy or pink for a girl? Whatever your choice of hue may be make sure it is also derived from paints that are zero- or low-VOC (volatile organic compounds) versions. These can be latex (water-based) paints or even those made of natural materials like clay. Today, these safer paints also come in a wide variety of color options. If your plans include any remodeling such as tearing down a wall, consider first that if your home was built before the 1980s, it likely contains highly toxic lead paint. In this case, it's wise to consult a contractor certified in lead abatement.

▶ **Choose Green Flooring:** Carpeting can contain a host of toxic chemicals that off-gas directly into your child's room, polluting the air they breathe. If new flooring is in your design plans, consider opting for healthier, green versions such as bamboo, cork, or natural wool carpeting. If the installation requires glues or other finishes, make sure you use those that are free of VOCs.

▶ **Steer Clear of PVC:** Products made with polyvinyl chloride plastic contain a host of harmful chemicals, including VOCs and phthalates, which can pollute the air quality in your child's room. If you have a window in their room that requires covering, install wood or metal versions instead of plastic roller shades. In lieu of harmful vinyl shower curtains, opt for healthy organic cotton or bamboo versions. Also, be sure to avoid any wallpaper made with PVC.

▶ **Consider Toxin-Free Furniture:** Much of today's furniture, even that made for nurseries or children's bedrooms, contains harmful pollutants such as formaldehyde and fire-retardant chemicals. Tests have actually shown that the latter, which have been linked to neurological and developmental impairments, learning disabilities, and cancer, are also present in baby products such as portable cribs, strollers, and high chairs. The best way to avoid these harmful elements in your home is to purchase products from companies that focus on creating healthy, green options. You can also check with product manufacturers to discern what goes into the items they produce.

▶ **Use Better Bedding:** When shopping for linens for your little ones, choose natural, un-dyed, untreated sheets. Permanent press and other treated products can contain formaldehyde that off-gasses into the air and is inhaled while children sleep.

Your children will be happy and healthy in a greener room. ©istockphoto.com/Galina Barskaya

Buying Safer Toys

IN RECENT YEARS, CHILDREN'S toys have been a hot topic of concern to parents across the country. In 2007, the discovery of a large number of toys made in China containing lead-based paints led several behemoth toy manufacturers to recall millions of toys. Lead is a serious neurotoxin and the paints that use it as an ingredient can easily be chipped off and ingested by a child.

Cost Meter:

But the ills of kids' playthings don't stop at lead. In fact, the consumer action guide, www.HealthyToys.org, lists the main chemicals of concern as lead, chlorine, cadmium, arsenic, and mercury. Sadly, there is little regulation to monitor, label, or eliminate these toxins from our children's toys.

Carcinogenic chlorine, which appears in toys made from petroleum-based PVC, has been detected in kids' products like plastic books, bibs, and backpacks plus plastic packaging and toys. Phthalates, an industrial group of chemicals that add flexibility and resilience to products, are also present in PVC. Even at low levels of exposure, phthalates are believed to cause hormone disruption, asthma, and breast cancer. A 2005 Centers for Disease Control study of the human population found that phthalates were present in almost everyone, with particularly high levels in children aged six to 11. While phthalates have been banned in toys and baby products in the European Union, Japan, and even the state of California, there continues to be no federal regulation by the U.S. government.

The heavy metal cadmium, which has been shown to cause developmental effects and is a known human carcinogen, has been found on painted toys and kids' PVC products like toys, lunch boxes, and bibs. Mercury, which has been found in vinyl backpacks and bath toys, affects the kidneys and is toxic to the nervous system.

Many plastic toys contain hormone-disrupting phthalates. ©istockphoto.com/mustafa

While the presence of chemicals in your child's toys may seem like an overwhelming concept to deal with, there are a few, simple steps you can take to create a healthier playtime. First off, you'll want to replace the PVC toys that they play with regularly; these could include bath toys, squeeze toys, and dolls.

When buying new toys, choose safer solid wood products, preferably unpainted, treated with non-toxic finishes. While the use of wood does deplete valuable trees from the planet, the products made from wood will be more durable and last longer than other types of toys, which end up in landfills faster.

Cloth and plush toys can also be safe options, as well as games and puzzles made of paper. If you are set on buying a soft plastic toy, be sure to verify that the product is phthalate-free.

For extra help with these issues, head to www.HealthyToys.org or www.greenpeace.org for product ratings, toy company report cards, and safety testing information. Past and present toy recall information is available through the Consumer Product Safety Commission website: http://www.cpsc.gov/cpscpub/prerel/prerel.html.

Green on the Cheap

The materials needed for kids' craft projects are also perpetrators in the chemical crime. Some glues and paints emit VOCs into the air and even crayons have been found to contain asbestos. For safer crafting, choose water-based paints, simple construction and scrap paper, and other natural options for your child.

Teaching Kids to Love and Respect the Planet

YOUR OWN CHILDREN—or those that are in your life via friends and family—will soak up the green knowledge you impart and take it forward with them in life. The earth is theirs for the future and their generation, with all their earth-friendly knowledge and acceptance of things like renewable energy and chemical-free foods, will likely take far better care of it than the past few generations have. These few tips and ideas will help you to teach your children well and sign them up for your green plan at home and beyond—and help you build memories that will last a lifetime.

▶ **Hold a green meeting:** Sit down with your children to discuss your desire to go green—if you present it in a fun way, they'll likely be excited about the unusual changes ahead. This is a great time to discuss plans like starting a recycling program and reducing energy usage at home.

▶ **Encourage them to reduce:** Their energy consumption is one of the best things they can reduce right away. If you have more than one child, you could even run a competition to see who is the best at turning off the lights in the rooms they leave throughout the day.

▶ **Motivate them to recycle:** If space permits, set up simple, clearly marked bins in the kitchen (i.e., "paper," "glass," "plastic") and challenge them to toss recyclables in the correct spot. You can also let them help set these items out on collection day.

Cost Meter: $0

▶ **Take them outside:** Let your kids experience the beauty of Mother Nature firsthand—take them hiking, canoeing, or sledding. Their outdoor adventures will make it quite clear why the earth is so worthy of preservation. They will also help promote a healthier, active lifestyle.

▶ **Design a garden:** If you have the space, build a garden for them to plant flowers or fruits and vegetables in your back yard. Nothing will solidify the beauty of nature's process more than watching something grow that they have planted. It will also underscore the delights of local, organic foods. If you live in an apartment or in the city, take them to a community garden where they can participate in the process.

▶ **Ride bikes together:** Teaching your child how to ride a bike is one of the best things you can do for the planet. This skill will stay with them always and may even inspire them to bike to school or work in the future.

A pinwheel perfectly demonstrates the force behind alternative energy. ©istockphoto.com/Izabela Habur

Eco Fact

A study by the Center for Environmental Health (CEH) found that a large number of children's soft vinyl lunch boxes contain high levels of lead, most of which is present in linings where this toxin can come into contact with food. To avoid this problem altogether, CEH recommends that parents buy products from those companies that have committed to sell only lead-safe lunch boxes. A few examples include Ingear, Fashion Accessory Bazaar, Lisa Frank, and Big Dogs.

How Conventional Pet Products Affect Pets... and Us

PETS ARE AN INTEGRAL PART of our society; they add warmth, dimension, and entertainment to our lives. In the U.S. alone, there are over 72 million dogs and nearly 82 million cats living in households across the country. In fact, households with dogs and cats outnumber those with children by 70 percent.

Even the numbers of birds in households range over 11 million and there are more than seven million horses. Americans also have a penchant for exotic pets: over 75 million fish, one million ferrets, nearly two million turtles, and half a million snakes live in U.S. households.

Over 43 million U.S. households are home to man's best friend. ©istockphoto.com/Eric Isselée

As much as we love our pets, we can take even better care of them by taking a deeper look at what's inside everything from their food to their toys. Unfortunately, the situation is much the same as it is with food and products for people—there are no current laws that require that the chemicals present in pet items be tested for safety. According to the EWG, the effects of these chemicals could be linked to the very high rate of cancer in dogs and hyperthyroidism in cats today.

A study conducted by the EWG of blood and urine samples from cats and dogs detected the presence of 48 industrial chemicals in the pets' bodies, most of which were at much higher levels than those typically found in humans. Fire retardants (PBDEs) were found at levels 23 times higher in cats than in people; cats' mercury levels were also five times higher. Perfluorochemicals (PFCs), which are stain- and grease-proofing chemicals, were 2.4 times higher in the dogs tested than what is typically detected in humans.

Why are man's best friends affected more significantly by chemical exposure? While pets are exposed to toxins in the same manner as humans—via the air they breathe and the tap water they drink and by being exposed to pesticides on lawns—they have smaller systems that, pound for pound, soak up more chemicals. They also operate closer to floors and lawns and, as a result, ingest a regular diet of chemicals.

Concerning toxins are also present in conventional pet foods, grooming products, and flea and tick controls like collars, shampoos, and sprays. These products rely on a family of chemicals called organophosphates, some of which have been banned from use in the past few years. Evidence exists that suggests these chemicals are not only harmful to pets but can also cause later-in-life effects, such as cancer and Parkinson's disease, for exposed children.

Again, it is your green choices that will protect the health and happiness of your pets at home. Limiting the toxins present in their environment plus choosing natural food, accessories, and pest controls is the best thing you can do for them. It is also a pledge to the planet to reduce your own use of chemicals that can pollute our waterways and air.

Is your pooch or feline being exposed to harmful chemicals via a flea collar? ©istockphoto.com/Li Kim Goh

Choosing Natural Pet Food Options

MANUFACTURED PET FOODS are typically packed with chemicals including supplements for fortification, flavor enhancers, and preservatives. They can also contain unnecessary fillers and by-products plus other questionable ingredients.

This truth came to light in 2007 when a pet food scare—and the resulting deaths of over 2,000 animals—was the cause of the largest recall in the history of the industry. More than 17,000 pets were sickened but the cause still remains in question. The pesticide aminopterin, a rat poison, was originally believed to be the cause; scientists later also found high levels of melamine, a chemical used in plastics and fertilizers, in wheat gluten found in the foods. Still, the EPA considers melamine of low potential risk.

Pet foods can contain some dubious ingredients.
©istockphoto.com/Mariya Bibikova

Cost Meter:

The food you feed your pet is of utmost importance for their development and continued health—it should deliver the nutrients they need in a safe package. As with your own food, one of the best moves you can make for your pet is to read their food labels. Since cats and dogs are carnivores, they require a meat-based diet packed with protein; this should be the first ingredient on the label.

In addition, avoid products that list by-products on the label; these are typically meat by-products like organs and other parts that are not fit for human consumption. Steer clear of additives that seem unnecessary, as well, like artificial colors, flavors, and chemical preservatives. Finally, remember that it's always a good idea to consult your veterinarian for purchasing advice when seeking out new dietary options for your pet.

Your local health food store and some veterinarian offices will carry all-natural pet foods that are better for your furry friends as well as the planet. The cost may be a little bit higher than conventional foods, but your vet bills may be lower in the long run.

Using Safer Flea Controls

L IKE PESTICIDES USED for your lawn and garden, those that are wrapped around your pet's neck or sprayed on their coats can contain a variety of ingredients that are harmful to them, you, and the planet. While the end result is counterintuitive to the intention, the flea and tick control business is a booming industry. According to Packaged Facts, over 30 percent of the 80 million households with dogs and/or cats living in them choose to use flea and tick controls such as flea collars and topical treatments.

The most offensive ingredient in flea control brews is a family of chemicals called organophosphates. Six of the seven members of this toxic tribe were removed from the market from 2000 to 2006 due to their effects on pets and people; these include chlorpyrifos, dichlorvos, phosmet, naled, diazinon, and malathion. Check your labels before using any flea product, especially if you've had it for some time, to confirm these elements are not present.

One organophosphate chemical, tetrachlorvinphos, is still in use in flea control products. Additionally, these products also use another family of chemicals called carbamates—the two most commonly used in pet products are carbaryl and propoxur. Both organophosphates and carbamates work against pests by interfering with the transmission of nerve signals. The problem is that these effects can also extend themselves to pets, children, and adults.

On the flip side, there are healthier, natural flea and tick control options that can also keep these chemicals from harming the planet:

▶ **Prevention is worth a pound of chemicals:** You can help your pet (and your family) avoid a flea problem in the first place by employing tactics like washing pet bedding once a week in hot water, vacuuming frequently, and using good grooming techniques. Keeping the grass in your lawn short and debris-free will also help to minimize the presence of pests.

▶ **Healthy diets repel pests:** You can also play offense by feeding your pet a healthy diet. With strong defenses, they are less likely to be attractive to fleas. A fish oil supplement will also help maintain your animal's healthy skin and coat.

▶ **Going back to basics:** If fleas make their presence known, your first line of defense is a basic flea comb. These are typically made of stainless steel and are specifically designed to remove fleas and eggs from your pet's hair.

▶ **The next step is organic:** If the problem persists, you can step things up to use a natural, organic flea bath combined with combing.

Selecting Safer Cat Litter

FOR FELINE OWNERS, cat litter is simply one of the unpleasant realities of daily life—cleaning, scooping, refilling. With over 37 million cat-owning households across the country, it's no wonder that cat litter sales rang in a whopping $730 million in 2002, according to Packaged Facts.

But this seemingly harmless, useful product actually hides an unhealthy secret. Today's ubiquitous litter variety is made of clay, which also happens to contain crystalline silica, a known human carcinogen. Clay cat litter also contains silica dust, which can cause respiratory irritation. Unfortunately, little research has been done to show the effects of these ingredients on cats and their owners.

Still, clay litter is a health concern and it also is produced via strip-mining processes that are anything but earth-friendly. Easy-to-use clumping cat litters have also come under scrutiny in the past few years as some claim that this product can be harmful to pets if ingested or inhaled because it solidifies inside their systems.

Move your felines away from litter varieties that may be harmful to their health, yours, and the planet's by choosing more natural, even organic, options. Eco- and health-conscious versions include those made from renewable plant resources like wood pellets, sawdust, barley, wheat, alfalfa, peanut hulls, or recycled newspaper. These items are often recycled from post-consumer waste, so you'll also be doing the earth a favor by reducing its workload.

Since over two million tons of litter lands in U.S. landfills each year, these biodegradable choices will also help reduce the world's waste burden. It is not recommended, however, that you compost your cat litter at home; parasites from your pet's waste can easily contaminate the compost you create, rendering it useless for garden or indoor plant applications.

Kittens are particularly vulnerable to the effects of clumping litter. ©istockphoto.com/Mark Hayes

Eco Fact

You can also green your pets by choosing to buy natural toys and accessories. Like children's plastic toys, pet options can also be made from PVC, which can be harmful to all animals. Pet parrots and exotic birds are especially vulnerable to the chemicals that are leached and off-gassed from soft PVC toys (i.e., lead and cadmium); these chemicals can be poisonous to them. Ask your veterinarian for the safest option and, when appropriate, opt for recycled toys and accessories like dye-free, organic hemp leashes.

Did You Know?

Cat waste can also be harmful to your health because it can spread toxoplasmosis, a serious parasitic disease that is transmitted through infected cat feces. Animals are typically infected by eating diseased meat, so outdoor cats are much more susceptible. It is estimated that over a third of the world's human population carry the toxoplasmosis virus. Pregnant women are at particular risk and should avoid handling cat litter or waste, because this disease can infect the fetus and cause miscarriage or severe birth defects. If you are pregnant and garden in an area that has outdoor cats, be sure to wear gloves to help protect you and your baby.

©istockphoto.com/TIM MCCAIG

Green Review:
How to Green Your Kids and Pets

Greening Your Children:

1. When you're expecting, try to avoid as many of the key, harmful chemicals outlined in this book as possible. When necessary, refer to the following chapters for relevant information:

   ▶ **Choosing natural cleaning products to clean up air quality: Chapter 3**

   ▶ **Buying pesticide-free organic foods and eating safer seafood: Chapter 5**

   ▶ **Using natural lawn care strategies to reduce pesticides and fertilizer exposure: Chapter 6**

   ▶ **Choosing natural personal care products to reduce chemical exposure: Chapter 8**

2. Buy a BPA-free baby bottle for your little one.

3. When preparing a nursery or redecorating a child's room, choose zero- or low-VOC paints, green flooring like bamboo or cork, toxin-free furniture (sans formaldehyde and fire-retardant chemicals), natural and organic bedding, and other products that do not contain PVC.

4. Toss any of your child's toys made of harmful PVC. When shopping for new toys, steer clear of those containing PVC or any other harmful chemicals. Refer to places like www.HealthyToys.org for more information.

5. Teach kids to love and respect the planet by instilling your green values in them—and inspiring them to choose earth-friendly activities like recycling, energy conservation, and biking.

Greening Your Pets:

1. Choose to feed your furry friends only natural (preferably organic) pet foods that do not contain harmful chemicals, preservatives, or animal by-products.

2. Ditch your pets' PVC toys and opt for natural, recycled playthings that are better for their health.

3. Review the labels of your flea control products and take anything that contains any of the banned organophosphates listed in this chapter to your local hazardous chemicals recycling center. Choose preventative methods and natural controls to maintain the health of your animal, your children, and yourself.

4. Switch your cat's litter to a natural, plant-based variety to protect the health of the planet and everyone in your household.

Five Ways to Go ÜberGreen

DOES YOUR ECO PASSION EXTEND beyond the pages of this book's eight-week plan? If so, you are not alone. The research firm Mintel has defined the "greenest" end of the consumer spectrum as "Super Greens," a group that it says tripled in size from late 2006 to early 2008. The results of its Green Living–U.S., February 2008 survey found that Super Greens are consumers "thoroughly committed to the 'green' lifestyle who almost always purchase green products." While this group is more likely to purchase earth-friendly items, their ties to eco-consciousness go way beyond consumerism— they view the green movement as a principled, ethical lifestyle choice. Are you Super Green?

Some Americans have even stepped beyond this boundary into lifestyles and choices that are extreme in their green-ness. *The New York Times* has coined the terms "carborexic" and "energy anorexic" for the members of this group, which isn't hesitant to live without heat or air conditioning, run vehicles on used cooking oil from local restaurants, aim for zero waste in their homes, and buy chickens to produce eggs that are as local as it gets.

While these measures may not be realistic for many people's lifestyles and living situations, there are numerous things you can do to live out your passion and become ÜberGreen. This chapter features five solid ways you can excel at greening your lifestyle and become even more committed to a healthy planet. Some of them are relatively simple, while others are decidedly life changing. A few are cost free, while others require a significant financial commitment upfront—one that will eventually pay for itself in energy and fuel savings. Read on for the scoop on these earth-friendly ideas.

Become an Activist

MERRIAM-WEBSTER DEFINES activism as "A doctrine or practice that emphasizes direct vigorous action especially in support of or opposition to one side of a controversial issue." The future of our planet—and how we approach it—is certainly a controversial issue today.

You don't have to attend a protest or chain yourself to a tree to be an activist—simply taking action to make things better and making your voice heard in your own community regarding green issues is activism. It is also being a responsible citizen of the earth.

You can make a huge difference by lobbying for things like better bike lanes, a more extensive recycling program, local foods served in schools, or greener business practices. How do you get started?

Step out from the crowd and spread your green ideas.
©istockphoto.com/Onur Döngel

Cost Meter: $0

The following steps will help launch you into your new role as activist.

▶ **Join a local group that advocates for the planet:** Do some web research to locate an organization in your area that champions green causes, from educating school kids about recycling to lobbying for green changes with the local government. Most groups welcome new volunteers; this is an excellent way to learn the ropes of activism in your area.

▶ **Write a letter—or 20:** Since the Letters to the Editor section of your local newspaper is likely the most-read page each day, this is an excellent spot for you to voice your aspirations for greening your local community. The members of your community will not be the only people informed of these ideas; local governments often have newspaper-clipping services that pull relevant topics for area politicians. Your letter-writing skills will also come in handy for campaigns directed to politicians. Persistence is a virtue in this endeavor; as letters pile up, bureaucrats tend to pay more attention. You could even go so far as to request an appointment with a local politician to review your ideas and concerns.

▶ **Share your ideas:** Discuss your green ideas with friends, family, and even strangers that you come into contact with. Keeping the concepts light and non-confrontational just may inspire them to change their own habits. If you find you have a number of people interested in making a particular change, such as making your town more bike-friendly, you could even set out to start a petition that could be presented to local politicians to illustrate the public's interest. These can be circulated door to door or via interested local merchants.

▶ **Go nationwide with online activism:** If your aspirations also lie beyond your local area, it's easy to take a national (or even international) tack with your ardor via green groups that have a strong online presence. A few places to start include the National Resources Defense Council (www.nrdc.org), the Environmental Working Group (www.ewg.org), www.stopglobalwarming.org, www.wecansolveit.org, and www.350.org.

Get a Green Collar Job

WOULD YOU LIKE TO WORK for an earth-conscious company? You can take your green enthusiasm and put it into play every day with a career that contributes to a better environment and a sustainable economy. There has never been a better time to make a career shift as green jobs are on the rise across America.

About 750,000 Americans now work in what are considered as "green jobs," including both extremely green occupations such as electric car engineers and solar project managers and traditional work in areas like sales, accounting, and marketing for truly green companies. The population of green workers is projected to skyrocket in the next 20 years, since green industries and the number of eco-conscious companies are on the rise.

Cost Meter: $0

Your career could help save the planet.
©istockphoto.com/kutay tanir

A 2008 United Nations report, entitled Green Jobs: Towards Decent Work in a Sustainable, Low-Carbon World, suggests that while a million people currently work in biofuels, that number could rise by another 12 million by 2030. Additionally, the report projected that the manufacture, installation, and maintenance of solar panels should add 6.3 million jobs by 2030 and wind power projects would require an additional two million workers.

The bottom line is that the development of green industries and the boom of green jobs will simply help build a more sustainable economy. The website, www.GreenJobsNow.com, suggests that in 2006 "renewable energy and energy efficiency technologies generated 8.5 million new jobs, nearly $970 billion in revenue, and more than $100 billion in industry profits."

At the presstime of this book, a proposal by president-elect Barack Obama heralded a promising economic plan to create new jobs via the development of alternative energies. The green collar movement is even happening at the state level—Minnesota Governor Tim Pawlenty has laid out a proposed "Green Jobs Investment Initiative" for his state, which is already at the forefront of alternative energy development.

How can you find a green job? The behemoth job-listing website www.monster.com boasts a targeted green career section that includes information on eco-friendly jobs. Other green job resources include www.greenjobs.com, www.environmentalcareer.com, and www.greenjobs.net. If you believe in the power of green jobs, you can also go to greenjobsnow.com and sign the petition to send a signal to our country's elected officials.

It is highly likely that your current experience and skill set can be applied to a green career; for example, construction workers can install solar panels and lawyers can work for clean-energy companies. Be sure to research the company you are interested in working for to ensure their green inclinations are more than marketing-fueled greenwashing. Once you have made the jump, you can head to work every day (by carpooling, biking, or taking mass transit, no doubt) knowing that you are making a real difference.

> "Be the change you want to see in the world.
>
> —Mahatma Gandhi

Buy a Hybrid or an Electric Vehicle

IF YOU'RE IN THE MARKET for a new vehicle or simply fed up with your car's fuel economy and resulting carbon emissions, it may be time to trade it in and trade up to a cleaner, greener automobile. Both hybrid and electric vehicles are excellent earth-friendly choices for your transportation needs; they may cost a bit more than a standard vehicle, but this upfront cost will ultimately be recouped in dollars saved at the fuel pump. Tax credits are also offered for the purchase of these low-emissions vehicles. It's clear that greener passenger vehicles are the wave of the future, so why not jump on the bandwagon?

The popular Toyota Prius hybrid vehicle gets approximately 48 mpg on the highway.
©istockphoto.com/TIM MCCAIG

Cost Meter: **$$$**
(over time, this change will save you money)

The Scoop on Hybrids

How They Work: Hybrid electric vehicles (HEVs) combine an internal combustion engine with an electric motor powered by batteries. The electric motor actually helps the conventional engine operate more efficiently, which ultimately cuts down on fuel use. On the flip side, the gasoline engine enables the HEV to travel long distances since the electric motor has a limited range. Most HEVs also employ regenerative braking, which uses the electric motor to stop the vehicle and, in turn, recovers and converts this kinetic energy into electricity to power the motor.

Pros: Most HEVs do not require a plug-in electrical charge, save for the plug-in hybrids, which have a range of about 20 miles on electricity alone before using any gasoline. They can attain a fuel economy of up to 45 to 55 mpg.

Cons: HEVs still run on gasoline, which burns fossil fuels and creates emissions, albeit less than conventional gas-powered vehicles.

What They Cost: Hybrids typically range from just over $21,000 to about $30,000, but luxury models can cost as much as $50,000 to $60,000.

Did You Know?

Politicians and business leaders in San Francisco have laid out a plan to make the Bay Area—including Silicon Valley— at the forefront of electric vehicle development by creating a vast network of battery charging stations. This proposed $250 million "refueling" infrastructure would be built by 2012 by Better Place, a company that has already reached agreements to do the same in Hawaii, Denmark, Israel, and Australia.

The Deal with EVs

How They Work: Electric Vehicles (EVs) are powered by electric motors and motor controllers rather than the standard internal combustion engine; the energy used to power the electric motor is derived from charged battery packs stored inside the vehicle. The EV market took off in the U.S. in the 1990s, but most of the vehicles manufactured then, which were sold under closed-end lease, were repossessed and destroyed. The first electric luxury sports car, the Tesla Roadster, was unveiled by Silicon Valley-based Tesla Motors in 2006—the concept behind this EV and consumers' desire for oil-free transportation has fueled a renewed interest in EVs. Expect to see an expanded offering in the coming years.

Pros: EVs deliver a quiet, fuel- and emissions-free ride.

Cons: These modern vehicles must be charged and the power to do so may come from a source that generates greenhouse gas emissions, unless you purchase clean electricity. Most also have a limited range on a single charge, save for the Tesla Roadster, which delivers about 220 miles of driving when fully charged.

What They Cost: While the Roadster rings in at $109,000, more affordable options are on the horizon. For example, the Chevy Volt, launching in 2011, will retail around $40,000.

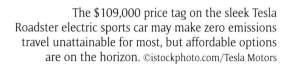

The $109,000 price tag on the sleek Tesla Roadster electric sports car may make zero emissions travel unattainable for most, but affordable options are on the horizon. ©istockphoto.com/Tesla Motors

Inspire—or Move to—a Transition Community

WOULD YOU LIKE TO LIVE in a community that embraces sustainable living and local resilience? Is it appealing to have like-minded, eco-conscious neighbors who desire to combat global warming and the potential effects of peak oil? If all this sounds appealing, then it might be time for you to move to a "transition town"—or start the movement towards this moniker in your own community.

The transition town movement was born out of a class project at Kinsale Further Education College in Kinsale, Ireland, where students worked with permaculture designer Rob Hopkins to write an "Energy Descent Plan." What they wrote together was a forward-thinking adaptation of their town's local systems, from energy production and economy to health and agriculture, which would lead it to energy independence and a more sustainable future.

One of the students, Louise Rooney, moved to present the plan to town councilors who made the historic decision to make Kinsale the world's first transition town. Hopkins, who has since written a tome entitled *The Transition Handbook*, returned to his hometown of Totnes, England, where the concept was embraced and expanded in 2006.

Cost Meter: $ to $$$$
(over time, this change will save you money)

Today, there are over 100 transition towns worldwide from Australia to Japan, including a number in the U.S. These currently include Boulder, CO, Sandpoint, ID, Ketchum, ID, Lyons, CO, Santa Cruz, CA, Montpelier, VT, and Portland, ME. According to the movement's website, www.transitiontowns.org, there are more than 600 additional communities considering the possibility of kicking off their own transition initiative, including over 100 in the U.S.

Transition towns aim to rely on locally supplied, sustainable energy. ©istockphoto.com/Vladimir

Despite the movement's name, any city, village, or small community can become a transition town. The main goal is to prepare and equip communities for the challenges and effects from climate change and peak oil. Transition towns set the goal to move, over a period of 10 to 20 years, from oil dependence to a low carbon diet. Transition towns also strive to develop ways to reduce the amount of energy they use—and to become more self-reliant.

One of the ways this is accomplished is the encouragement of reciprocal exchange of goods and services to fuel the local economy; some towns, such as Totnes, have even developed their own currency. Transition towns also focus on developing local, sustainable energy sources, growing food in community gardens, selling and buying locally grown produce, and matching waste from one business with another operation that can use it.

Is your town on the list of those considering the transition to a more sustainable, locally focused mode of operation? If so, perhaps you could join in the excitement by contacting the local organizers. If not, maybe you yourself could inspire this change locally. Or, if all else fails, you could always move to a transition town and join in this groundbreaking movement. For more information on how to inspire a transition town, see www.transitiontowns.org.

Buy, Build, or Remodel a Green Home

LIVING IN A GREEN HOME that generates its own energy, including everything from electricity to heat, is more possible today than ever before. Green builders have cropped up across the country to deliver earth-friendly designs that suit your eco passions; many will also build to your own specifications.

In addition, the prevalence of green building contractors and suppliers has helped lower costs in the past few years. In fact, a 2008 study sponsored by the U.S. Green Building Council found that building green costs an average of 2.5 percent more upfront than conventional building.

Cost Meter: **$ $ $ $**
(over time, this change will save you money)

In the long run, building green will ultimately result in cost savings related to energy and water conservation features. The study also found that green homes would have a median energy savings of 33 percent a year. Given these numbers, it appears homeowners that buy or build green would recoup their investment quickly.

Building green only costs about 2.5 percent more upfront. ©istockphoto.com/Richard Schmidt-Zuper

If you're in the market for a new home, buying or building your own eco-conscious abode is an honorable commitment to make to the planet. It will reduce your use of precious resources along with putting a cap on your carbon emissions. The Commission for Environmental Cooperation estimates that if there was a rapid uptake of available and emerging energy-saving technologies in home building in North America, it could result in the reduction of 1,711 megatons of CO_2 emissions. In addition, your green home will also be a healthier one for its inhabitants, since it will likely feature low-VOC paints, better air ventilation, and other "cleaner" finishings.

In some cases, it may even be greener (or necessary) to buy a used home and retrofit it with green accoutrements like solar panels, solar hot water, a wind turbine, geothermal heating, or on-demand hot water. If you're not about to move from your current home, many of these switches can be made with some planning and an upfront cost investment. Your payback should be relatively quick in energy savings and tax credits, which are currently available for energy-savvy home upgrades like solar panels and ENERGY STAR windows.

Building and renovating green is a building movement that is picking up speed. A McGraw-Hill Construction Analytics report on the global green building industry found that 53 percent of respondents expect to be dedicated to going green on more than 60 percent of their projects in the next five years. For more information on buying green, building green, or finding a green builder in your area, check out www.greenhomesforsale.com, www.greenhomeguide.org, or http://directory.greenbuilder.com/search.gbpro.

Eco Fact

According to the Environmental Protection Agency, in the U.S., buildings account for:

- **40 percent of total energy use**

- **12 percent of total water consumption**

- **68 percent of total electricity consumption**

- **38 percent of total carbon dioxide emissions**

- **60 percent of total non-industrial waste generation**

Green Review: Ways to Go ÜberGreen

1. Become an activist.

2. Get a greencollar job.

3. Buy a hybrid or an electric vehicle.

4. Inspire—or move to—a transition community.

5. Buy, build, or remodel a green home.

Glossary

Bamboo Fiber: a fiber derived from bamboo plants, which have a built-in natural defense against bacteria and, thus, do not require pesticides to grow abundantly. This natural feature is also translated into the bamboo fiber, which boasts anti-bacterial as well as odor-resistant and hypoallergenic qualities.

Carbon Emissions: the release of carbon dioxide into the atmosphere, which is caused primarily by the burning of fossil fuels. Usually measured in metric tons, CO_2 emissions play a key role in trapping heat in the earth's atmosphere, an event that leads to global warming.

Climate Change: the reported increase in the average measured temperature of the earth's surface air and oceans. From 1905 to 2005, this average temperature rose by 1.33 degrees Fahrenheit. The Intergovernmental Panel on Climate Change has concluded that this change is due to the increased levels of greenhouse gases in the atmosphere, the majority of which are due to human activities that burn fossil fuels.

Community Supported Agriculture (CSA): a community of individuals that each pledges a set amount of money to support a local farm for the growing season. This membership helps cover the farmer's anticipated costs of operation and entitles members to a specified amount of fresh produce on a weekly basis. This system builds a unique consumer-producer relationship.

Composting: a process that utilizes organic material such as food scraps and yard trimmings, which are disposed of and mixed in a compost bin to produce naturally nutrient-rich and toxin-free soil for projects such as landscaping or agriculture. Because it eliminates a waste stream, composting also helps keep trash out of landfills.

EcoTourism: a form of tourism that is attractive to eco-conscious and socially conscious travelers, it focuses on responsible travel to natural areas. An ecotourism vacation aims to minimize the negative aspects associated with conventional travel by encouraging earth-friendly tactics and promoting local economies with travel dollars.

Electric Vehicle (EV): a vehicle powered by electric motors and motor controllers instead of an internal combustion engine. The energy used to power the electric motor is derived from charged battery packs stored inside the vehicle. These clean, emissions-free vehicles are coming onto the transportation landscape; expect to see more options launched in the coming years.

Energy Audit: an assessment of a home's energy efficiency that also provides tips and strategies to reduce the amount of energy that the home consumes. Today, both do-it-yourself audits and those performed by a qualified energy audit professional are available. Energy audits also save money in the long run by lowering utility bills.

ENERGY STAR: the international standard for energy-efficient consumer products, which was developed by the U.S. Environmental Protection Agency in 1992. The roster of ENERGY STAR products ranges from major appliances to office equipment and home electronics. The ENERGY STAR program has also developed energy performance rating systems for several commercial and institutional building types and manufacturing facilities.

Environmental Estrogens: chemical compounds found in the pesticides, plastics, and detergents that can cause major changes in endocrine cells. More than 60 substances, including dioxin and PCB, have been identified as environmental estrogens.

Farmer's Market: these markets, which are growing in numbers in the U.S., feature items from farms within the local region. They typically carry a wide variety of produce, eggs, and meats, much of which is produced organically.

Fertilizers: a substance or mixture that promotes plant growth. Fertilizers are composed of either organic matter (i.e., compost) or inorganic chemicals or minerals. High concentrations of chemical fertilizers threaten public health and the world's ecosystems while also increasing greenhouse gas emissions.

Fluoridated Water: water that is supplemented naturally or by government agencies to contain fluoride. Fluoride compounds are found naturally in some groundwater supplies, but the U.S. has added chemical fluoride ions into drinking water with the intentions of reducing tooth decay since the 1940s. While toxic at moderate to high doses, fluoride can be beneficial for dental health in low doses. The general level of fluoride in drinking water is supposed to range from 0.7–1.2 parts per million.

Fossil Fuel: a combustion fuel source such as coal, natural gas, and crude oil that has been created by the compression and heating of ancient organic remains underneath the earth's surface. Fossil fuels are a non-renewable resource which, when burned, cause the emission of carbon dioxide and other greenhouse gases into the atmosphere. Approximately 90 percent of U.S. greenhouse gas emissions come from the combustion of fossil fuels.

Free Farmed: a designation set up by the American Humane Association as part of the first animal welfare certification program in the U.S. Free Farmed is now referred to as American Humane Certified™ on verified products; it denotes that certified producers' care and handling of animals meets the standards of American Humane Association (i.e., animals are raised with appropriate space and without antibiotics).

Genetically Engineered (GE) Cotton: a plant type introduced in the 1990s by agricultural giants Calgene and Monsanto that is created by splicing foreign genetic material into plant genomes. GE cotton is a new organism that is not present in the natural world. It boasts built-in pest defenses derived from Bacillus Thuringiensis (Bt), which is present in every cell of the engineered plant. Bt, however, may leach into soil, harming soil microorganisms and threatening soil ecology.

Grass Fed: a designation for livestock products that denotes animals were given continuous access to natural pastures for an extended amount of time prior to processing. Compared to meat from conventional feedlot cattle, grass-fed cattle meat has been shown to be lower in fat, saturated fat, cholesterol, and calories.

Green Jobs: a wide range of jobs that apply environmentally conscious concepts to improve conservation and sustainability both locally and globally. A growing number of people around the world work in what are considered "green jobs," including both extremely green occupations such as wind turbine project managers and traditional work in areas like accounting for green companies.

Greenhouse Gases: gases emitted from both naturally occurring and human-caused sources that absorb infrared radiation in the atmosphere. These gases, which include water vapor, carbon dioxide, methane, nitrous oxide, ozone, and CFCs, are responsible for maintaining the earth's temperature. An overabundance of greenhouse gases in the atmosphere creates the "greenhouse effect," an event that contributes to global warming.

Greenwashing: a term used to describe the act of a company, an organization, or an individual that has misled consumers into thinking they participate in healthy environmental practices or produce "green" products or services to gain a marketing advantage.

Groundwater: up to 20 percent of the earth's freshwater is stored under the ground surface in forms such as aquifers, soil moisture, permafrost, and geothermal formations. Groundwater is most commonly threatened by pollutants that can leach into this supply and make it unsafe.

Hemp Fiber: a naturally soft fiber that is also mold and mildew resistant, hemp was the first plant to be cultivated for use in making cloth and clothing. Hemp is incredibly fast growing and requires little to no pesticides or herbicides to grow. Industrial hemp is used to manufacture everything from clothing and textiles to paper and foods.

Herbicide: a chemical pesticide designed to control or destroy plants, weeds, or grasses. Some herbicides can cause negative health effects as well as contaminate groundwater sources.

Hybrid Electric Vehicle (HEV): a hybrid vehicle that combines an internal combustion engine with an electric motor powered by batteries. The electric motor helps the conventional engine operate more efficiently and cut down on fuel use. At the same time, since the electric motor has a limited range, the gasoline engine allows the HEV to travel longer distances.

Hydroelectric Power: the production of power through the use of the gravitational force of falling or flowing water. The kinetic energy created by the movement of water flowing downstream is converted into electricity via a hydroelectric power plant. Here, water (which is typically held at a dam) is forced through a turbine connected to a generator to create energy.

Hypermilers: a group of drivers that employ specific driving techniques to attain a vehicle's ultimate gas mileage. Not necessarily legal and not always safe, these techniques include minimizing braking, drafting freight trucks, and using downhills to gain added momentum for uphills. Some estimate they can achieve up to 50 mpg and more in average vehicles (i.e., non-hybrid) by hypermiling.

Insecticides: a substance or mixture in the form of a pesticide that is intended to destroy insects in any developmental stage. Used primarily in agriculture, insecticides can alter ecosystems, leach into groundwater, and increase the risk of health issues for humans. Some insecticides have been banned for such reasons.

Kilowatt Hours (kWh): delivered by electric utilities, this unit of energy is equal to that which is expended by one kilowatt in one hour.

Landfill Gas (LFG): a methane gas that is born as the solid waste of a landfill decomposes under anaerobic conditions. LFG can be captured, converted, and used as an energy source. This act helps prevent methane from making its way into the atmosphere as a climate-changing greenhouse gas.

Lead Paint: paint that contains lead, a dangerous substance known to cause nervous system damage, hearing loss, kidney damage, and reproductive problems. Children under the age of six are more susceptible to its hazards because their systems are still developing. Leaded paint was banned from residential use in the U.S. in 1978, but it still remains in many older homes.

Local Food: a term that refers to food that is produced within a limited range of the purchaser's home via local farms and producers. A local food movement has risen up in the U.S., where grocery store-bought produce is shipped an average of 1,500 miles from the farm where it was produced, using an enormous amount of fossil fuels along the way.

Methane: a major component of the natural gas used in homes, methane is an abundant fuel produced by the anaerobic decomposition of organic compounds. At room temperature and standard pressure it is a colorless, odorless, and non-toxic gas.

Methane Emissions: the potent greenhouse gas produced when methane is burned as a fuel. These emissions, which are a result of activities such as fossil fuel production and waste management, have a higher, short-term effect on global warming than carbon dioxide emissions of the same mass.

Organic Cotton: cotton that is grown organically without the use of pesticides or fertilizers and from plants that are not genetically modified. Its production focuses on maintaining soil fertility and limiting environmental impact on the earth. Organic cotton is certified by the USDA National Organic Program.

Organic Pollutants: contaminants in the environment that can pose adverse effects to human health and the environment. Common organic pollutants are found in insecticides, fungicides, and the PCBs used in making plastics.

Peak Oil: the point at which many experts believe the world will reach "peak oil" production, after which petroleum extraction will begin to decline. U.S. oil production peaked in the 1970s. While a 2008 report by the International Energy Agency determined peak oil would not occur until at least 2030, a large number of scientists believe that oil supplies are already in decline.

Pesticides: a substance or mixture that repels or destroys pests or is used as a plant defoliant or desiccant. Synthetic pesticides have raised public concern due to their potential toxicity for humans, animals, and the environment. In most countries, pesticides are regulated by government agencies but still remain a major health concern.

Petroleum Distillates: a petroleum-based chemical found in a wide variety of consumer products, including furniture polish and lip gloss, that contribute to air pollution and can cause nerve damage and eye irritation. Pesticides and fertilizers can also contain petroleum distillates.

Polyvinyl Chloride (PVC): an inexpensive and extremely durable plastic that is found in a large number of consumer products, including children's toys, food wrappers, and shower curtains. PVC also accounts for over 50 percent of the materials used in building construction. Additives, such as phthalate plasticizers, are added to soften PVC but these have been found to leach and cause health problems such as liver damage and endocrine disruption.

Slow Travel: a travel concept that focuses on staying in one location and enjoying its highlights, including the local people, shops, culture, and food. The slow travel movement is an offshoot of the slow food movement, which was born in Italy as a protest in the 1980s when McDonald's opened in Rome.

Sodium Hydroxide: otherwise known as lye, this chemical is used in the manufacture of many household items, such as soaps, detergents, drain cleaners, and oven cleaners. It can cause extreme irritation to eyes, nose, and throat and burn skin tissue directly upon contact.

Solar Power: the conversion of light and radiant heat from the sun into electricity. Solar power converts the power of the sun's light into energy via photovoltaic systems (where wafers made of silicon react to the sun to create electricity) and solar-thermal technologies, which use mirrors to heat a liquid that produces steam used to generate electricity. Many homes and buildings use this alternative form of energy; solar "farms" are also cropping up across the country.

Staycation: a vacation taken while staying at home and relaxing or one involving day trips in the vacationer's home area. The staycation trend was born out of economy-troubled Americans' desire to take less expensive and less stressful vacations.

Transition Town: a socially conscious movement born out of a class project at Kinsale Further Education College in Kinsale, Ireland, where students worked with professor Rob Hopkins to write a forward-thinking adaptation of their town's local systems, from energy production to economy, which would lead it to energy independence and a more sustainable future. The town adopted this concept, which has also spread around the globe to other communities. Today, there are over 100 transition towns worldwide, including several in the U.S.

Virgin Fiber: wood fiber from trees that has never been used before in the manufacture of paper or other products. Products made from virgin fiber often have the potential to be made from recycled, post-consumer products instead.

Volatile Organic Compounds (VOCs): harmful organic chemical compounds that are capable of vaporizing and entering the air supply, thus causing harm to human health. Examples of artificial VOCs include paint, paint thinners, and dry cleaning solvents.

Wind Power: the conversion of wind energy into a renewable energy such as electricity. Wind turbines scoop up wind with two or three long blades; the movement of the turbine is converted, through a generator, into electricity. Wind power is a sustainable alternative to non-renewable fossil fuels that can also help reduce greenhouse gas emissions.

Xeriscaping: the practice of landscaping in ways that do not require supplemental irrigation, such as the use of plants with water needs that are appropriate to the particular climate in which they are grown. Xeriscaping practices also reduce the amount of evaporation and runoff created during watering.

Index

transequation (continued)

transportation *(continued)*
  hybrid vehicle, 203–204
  idling, 157
  octane level, 159
  oil supply, 155–156
  public transit, 161–162
  SmartWay designation, 167
  telecommunication, 160
travel. *See also* **transportation**
  air, 170–171
  ecotourism, 174–175
  foregoing costs and stresses with, 172
  slow travel movement, 173
  supporting green business through, 176–178
  volunteer vacations, 181
TRCs (Tradable Renewable Certificates), 68
trees, 29
triclosan, 138

U

Union Square Greenmarket, 91
U.S. Department of Energy
  green utility programs, 61
  Home Energy Save audit, 72
U.S. Geological Survey, 2
utility programs, green, 61

V

vacation. *See* **travel**
vegetables, 82
vehicle. *See* **transportation**
ventilation, household environment, 33
vermicomposting, 111
VOCs (volatile organic compounds), 32
volunteer vacations, 181

W

waste. *See* **garbage**
water
  antibiotics in, 92
  clean drinking, 92–93
  conserving, 44
  drought conditions, 42
  eco-conscious lifestyle changes, 27
  filtration systems, 18, 93
  herbicides in, 92
  inorganic contaminants in, 92
  lawn care, 107–108
  lead in, 92–93
  leaky faucets, 44
  microbial contaminants in, 92
  pesticides in, 92
  quality reports, 93
  radio active contaminants in, 92
  reusable water bottles, 17–18, 93
  showers, limiting time in, 27, 44
  water-efficient appliances, 42, 44
Water Partners International, 27
weed control, lawn care, 105–106
wet cleaning clothing, 132
wildlife, ingestion and entanglement of plastic, 14
wind power
  eco-conscious lifestyle changes, 21–22
  pros and cons, 60
wool, 125–126
World Health Organization, 32

X–Y

xeriscaping, 106

yard. *See* **lawn care**